Poetry with a Sharper Edge

**Educational edition edited by David Orme
and Neil MacRae**

abridged from *Poetry with an Edge*
edited by Neil Astley
(Bloodaxe Books)

Stanley Thornes (Publishers) Ltd

This edition published in 1990 by:
Stanley Thornes (Publishers) Ltd
Old Station Drive
Leckhampton
CHELTENHAM   GL53 0DN
England

British Library Cataloguing in Publication Data
Poetry with a sharper edge.
1. Poetry in European languages – Anthologies
I. MacRae, Neil   II. Orme, David   III. Poetry with an edge
808.81
ISBN 0–7487–0500–7

Printed and bound in Great Britain at The Bath Press, Avon

Contents

iii

Preface

There are few exciting collections of poetry for those students who want to explore English beyond Key Stage 4, but this is one! The poems here have all been chosen because they have something to say and, as such, they all stand on their own merits.

We did not want to clutter up the anthology with ideas for work but rather encourage students to explore their own ideas for themes and comparisons as they read the poems. Nevertheless, some ideas for related work have been given at the end of this preface.

The scope of Advanced Level English is broadening: some syllabuses are changing and a number of examination boards are beginning to introduce elements of coursework and creative writing.

Instead of just coping with tricky exam questions, students may now have the opportunity to write at length, study a wider range of written forms, look at plays as performances, write personal responses to a novel and even produce their own poetry. Very often these changes are accompanied by a new kind of an examination question too: personal responses are often derived and these encourage a far greater sensitivity towards language. It is this engagement with writing which we hope will be further encouraged by *Poetry with a Sharper Edge* and that enjoyment of the poems will lead to vigorous, creative responses from students.

Working with the poems

It is often difficult to communicate that sense of achievement which the poet experiences as a poem grows, develops and takes its final shape.

When the reader first meets the poem everything can look very neat and tidy: there are no loose ends, no misshapen bulges and the text has settled into its meaning like a piece of bespoke clothing.

What is there now left for the reader to do? To get back to the struggling with words that shaped the poem, other approaches are needed. Poems can be deconstructed to allow subtleties of structure and meaning to reappear. Deletions of words or phrases, the title or whole stanzas may allow useful discussion. Similarly, the text might be more radically altered:

whole sections of a poem could be cut up for rearrangement by students or a key section of the poem used as a starting point for "brain-storming" discussion and speculation about directions the poem might take.

The poems in this anthology are arranged chronologically according to the poet's date of birth. Students should, however, discover ideas and structures which link several poems. Exploring these may offer new insights into the individual poems. For example, there are obvious points of cross-reference in Brendan Kennelly's 'Nails' and the Belfast poems of Ciarán Carson (p. 51). Several poems concern the deaths of animals while others have clear structural links.

More exciting than this is to experiment with writing original poems that imitate techniques: for example, creating your own poem using film dialogue (see Ken Smith's 'Bogart in the dumb waiter' p. 27). Each poet in this collection wrestled hard over words and ideas before the final version appeared on paper. Students can get closer to the heart of this process by writing their own questions on the text or sorting out contentious statements provided by others.

Finally, we shouldn't forget non-written responses. Talking to different audiences about the poems and drawing or sketching ideas which spring from the text will allow new insights to develop. The relationship between poetry and the visual imagery of photographs, paintings, film and television should not be underestimated. Why not produce a storyboard or photographic collage, as a personal response to some poems? Anything is possible, provided the excitement remains and that *Poetry with a Sharper Edge* is enjoyed!

Neil Macrae

January 1990

Foreword

When I started reading contemporary poetry, I nearly gave up. I'd read a few modern poets at school, and after getting hold of books by poets such as Ted Hughes and Philip Larkin, I looked around to find out what else there was. I didn't get very far.

My local bookshop didn't stock much poetry. They said there wasn't much demand for it. Browsing through the shelves, I wasn't surprised. The poetry books looked rather dull for a start. The blurbs were written in that wooden, academic style: they didn't make me want to read the books, they put me off. Poets were called the Author: the biographical notes usually said that the Author lived in London and he'd read English at Oxbridge. The Author didn't write poetry, he wrote *verse*. He was always English, and rarely female. I wasn't impressed.

This was the early 1970s, but the world of the slim volume of verse, with its dusty air of worthiness, seemed more like some relic of the 1950s. This impression was reinforced when I started trying to read these writers. Most of their poems left me cold, but because they were Famous Authors I gave them the benefit of the doubt, blaming my own ignorance of contemporary poetry. I was convinced that I was missing something, and that there must be something at fault with my response, but much as I tried I couldn't see how their work could communicate much to anyone. To me, they were just boring, and their poetry was either second-hand or second-rate; dull, unimaginative, self-regarding or pseudo-intellectual. Either way it was boring.

I couldn't think of anyone who would find this stuff at all interesting, and couldn't understand how anyone had thought it worth publishing; or how books like these could be produced by reputable publishers. I should have trusted my first response.

I wouldn't have read much further had I not also discovered a few of the newer poets who were just then being published for the first time, such as Seamus Heaney, Derek Mahon, Tony Harrison and Douglas Dunn, and major European poets such as Zbigniew Herbert, Miroslav Holub and Joseph Brodsky, whose books were curiously hard to obtain. Even in translation, the Europeans communicated far more than most of the English poets I'd come across. They weren't concerned with how things looked, but how things *were*; like the English Metaphysicals, they were obsessed with ideas and human experience, not appearances.

However, my excitement at finally discovering some poets whose work meant something to me was tempered by feelings of annoyance, frustration and disbelief that their books had been so difficult to find. Moreover, many of the European poets were no longer published in English, and their books were only available – if you were lucky – from libraries or secondhand bookshops. And if that was the fate of some of the most outstanding poets of the century, what of all the other poets I might also want to read?

I started asking questions. Through becoming involved with a literary magazine, and then in helping to organise some poetry readings, I came across poets who couldn't get anyone to publish their work, and not because it wasn't any good. I couldn't understand why it was that their poetry meant much more to me than a lot of the stuff I was reading in books.

It wasn't an easy connection to make. Do you question why the books you read *exist* as books? Books don't appear spontaneously: they all start out as typescripts. You probably realise that they have to be printed, that someone has to turn them into books, but before that happens, someone – a publisher – has to decide which books are worth printing.

It's easier with the classics, where the publishers just reprint books by the great writers of the past. Yet while their work has stood the test of time, their reputations have often been earned posthumously. William Blake was viewed as an eccentric engraver by his contemporaries, and the few people who'd read his poetry thought it was laughable nonsense; like Emily Dickinson (unpublished in her lifetime), he was many years in the grave before he was recognised as one of the greatest poets in the English language. Wordsworth too was at first regarded as a minor talent, and when he visited London the literary people ridiculed him for his thick Cumbrian accent. In the early 19th century, when Wordsworth, Coleridge and Keats were writing their best work, the most popular and critically acclaimed poets were Campbell, Moore and Southey (and later, Byron). Who's heard of Campbell, Moore and Southey today?

Today, in Britain alone, there are thousands and thousands of people who write novels, short stories, poetry and plays, but fewer than one per cent of those are ever published as books. From those hundreds of thousands of typescripts, the publishers pick out the ones they think are good and which they think they'll be able to sell because people will want to read them.

Who decides what's good? With new writing, it's the editor employed by the publishers. I decided that in the case of much of the poetry I was reading, the editors had got it wrong. So I borrowed some money and set up my own publishing house, and called it Bloodaxe Books (after the Viking king Eric Bloodaxe). Ten years (and 100 books) later, the *Sunday Times* commented, giving Bloodaxe its annual publisher's award: 'Bloodaxe Books has established a ferocious reputation as a publisher of ground-breaking modern poetry. It has cornered a market in the publishing industry with flair, imagination and conspicuous success.' And yet none of this would have happened but for the poetry itself: and because the poets had something to say, because I trusted my own judgement, and because readers have liked the books, many of which wouldn't otherwise have been published at all.

My test of a good poem is that it must *give* something to the reader. Housman said it had to lift the hairs on the back of his neck. Keats said it should 'strike the reader as the wording of his own highest thoughts, and appear almost a remembrance'. This kind of response is what I'd call *edge*. A good poem will always startle the reader.

This book is based on a larger "sampler" anthology called *Poetry with an Edge* containing work by most of the British, Irish, American and European poets Bloodaxe has published. It's been produced by another publisher, Stanley Thornes, whose editors David Orme and Neil MacRae have had the very difficult task of honing it down into *Poetry with a Sharper Edge*. This book wouldn't exist – and you wouldn't be holding it in your hands now – if I hadn't decided to publish books by all these poets (out of all the thousands who send me work each year) because their poetry spoke directly to me. Poetry should communicate in this way, person to person, and I hope you'll find at least some of these poems will strike a chord in you too.

As with music and art, poetry has to be well crafted if it's any good, but there are many different kinds of poets, all with their own individual voices and writing styles. I don't expect you'll like them all, any more than you'll like all the records in the top 20, or all the paintings in your local art gallery. If there are particular poets you really like, you can read more of them in their own books, which you'll find listed at the beginning of each section. But give them all a chance. Approach each poet with an open mind, and trust your own judgement.

Neil Astley

Editor, Bloodaxe Books

Martin Bell

MARTIN BELL was born in 1918 in Hampshire. He was a prominent member of 'The Group' in London during the 50s, and a major influence on younger poets like Peter Redgrove and Peter Porter. His poetry reached a wide audience during the 60s through *Penguin Modern Poets*, and in 1967 he published his *Collected Poems 1937-1966*, his first and last book. He died in poverty in Leeds in 1978.

Selection from: *Complete Poems* (1988), edited by Peter Porter.

Like other "provincial" working-class contemporaries, Bell wrote fantastical, highly erudite, biting, belligerent poetry. And yet – as Philip Hobsbaum said – he also wrote 'some of the most delicate love poems of our time' as well as 'one of the major war poems in the language'. ●

From Ode to Groucho

What you had was a voice
To talk double-talk faster,
Twanging hypnotic
In an age of nagging voices –
And bold eyes to dart around
As you shambled supremely,
Muscular moth-eaten panther!

Black eyebrows, black cigar,
Black painted moustache –
A dark code of elegance
In an age of nagging moustaches –
To discomfit the coarse mayor,
Un-poise the suave headmaster,
Reduce all the old boys to muttering fury.

A hero for the young,
Blame if you wish the human situation –
Subversivest of con-men
In an age of ersatz heroes:
Be talkative and shabby and
Witty; bully the bourgeois;
Act the obvious phoney.

Reasons for Refusal

Busy old lady, charitable tray
Of social emblems: poppies, people's blood –
I must refuse, make you flush pink
Perplexed by abrupt No-thank-you.
Yearly I keep up this small priggishness,
Would wince worse if I wore one.
Make me feel better, fetch a white feather, do.

Everyone has list of dead in war,
Regrets most of them, e.g.

Uncle Cyril; small boy in lace and velvet
With pushing sisters muscling all around him,
And lofty brothers, whiskers and stiff collars;
The youngest was the one who copped it.
My mother showed him to me,
Neat letters high up on the cenotaph
That wedding-caked it up above the park,
And shadowed birds on Isaac Watts' white shoulders.

And father's friends, like Sandy Vincent;
Brushed sandy hair, moustache, and staring eyes.
Kitchener claimed him, but the Southern Railway
Held back my father, made him guilty.
I hated the khaki photograph,
It left a patch on the wallpaper after I took it down.

Others I knew stick in the mind,
And Tony Lister often –
Eyes like holes in foolscap, suffered from piles,
Day after day went sick with constipation
Until they told him he could drive a truck –
Blown up with Second Troop in Greece:
We sang all night once when we were on guard.

And Ken Gee, our lance-corporal, Christian Scientist –
Everyone liked him, knew that he was good –
Had leg and arm blown off, then died.
Not all were good. Gross Corporal Rowlandson

Fell in the canal, the corrupt Sweet-water,
And rolled there like a log, drunk and drowned.
And I've always been glad of the death of Dick Benjamin,
A foxy urgent dainty ball-room dancer –
Found a new role in military necessity
As R.S.M. He waltzed out on parade
To make himself hated. Really hated, not an act.
He was a proper little porcelain sergeant-major –
The earliest bomb made smithereens:
Coincidence only, several have assured me.

In the school hall was pretty glass
Where prissy light shone through St George –
The highest holiest manhood, he!
And underneath were slain Old Boys
In tasteful lettering on whited slab –
And, each November, Ferdy the Headmaster
Reared himself squat and rolled his eyeballs upward,
Rolled the whole roll-call off an oily tongue,
Remorselessly from A to Z.

Of all the squirmers, Roger Frampton's lips
Most elegantly curled, showed most disgust.
He was a pattern of accomplishments,
And joined the Party first, and left it first,
At OCTU won a prize belt, most improbable,
Was desert-killed in '40, much too soon.

His name should burn right through that monument.

No poppy, thank you.

Denise Levertov

DENISE LEVERTOV was born in 1923 and grew
up in Ilford, Essex. In 1948 she moved to the
States, and during the next three decades
established herself as 'America's foremost
contemporary woman poet' *(Library Jour-
nal)*. She also became a prominent political
activist, campaigning for civil rights, against
the Vietnam War and against the Bomb. 'We
are living our whole lives in a *state of
emergency*,' she wrote in 1967.
    Her books are published by New Direc-
tions in America, and by Bloodaxe in Britain.

Selection from: *Selected
Poems* (1986).

The Mutes
from SELECTED POEMS

Those groans men use
passing a woman on the street
or on the steps of the subway

to tell her she is a female
and their flesh knows it,

are they a sort of tune,
an ugly enough song, sung
by a bird with a slit tongue

but meant for music?

Or are they the muffled roaring
of deafmutes trapped in a building that is
slowly filling with smoke?

Perhaps both.

Such men most often
look as if groan were all they could do,
yet a woman, in spite of herself,

knows it's a tribute:
if she were lacking all grace
they'd pass her in silence:

so it's not only to say she's
a warm hole. It's a word

in grief-language, nothing to do with
primitive, not an ur-language;
language stricken, sickened, cast down

in decrepitude. She wants to
throw the tribute away, dis-
gusted, and can't,

it goes on buzzing in her ear,
it changes the pace of her walk,
the torn posters in echoing corridors

spell it out, it
quakes and gnashes as the train comes in.
Her pulse sullenly

had picked up speed,
but the cars slow down and
jar to a stop while her understanding

keeps on translating:
'Life after life after life goes by

without poetry,
without seemliness,
without love.'

G.F. Dutton

Selection from: *Squaring the Waves* (1986).

GEOFFREY FRASER DUTTON was born in 1924. He has spent most of his life in Scotland, whose passionate austerities, urban or otherwise, edge much of his poetry. His numerous books cover many subjects, from enzymology to mountaineering.

'Over a huge landscape – recognisably Scotland and its border of cold ocean – Dutton's strong, clean poems strike like shafts of light through rolling clouds. They are illuminations. Each poem exists in an enormous perspective of time...I think he is one of the finest poets of our time' – Anne Stevenson. ●

idyll

the engine on the bank
pumps water. it is intent,
hunched in its cycles. smoke

and stuttering enamel
have constructed a great silence.
they have disposed

the evening; they are sufficient.
the river flows past glittering.
the pipeline vanishes into the forest.

not far away in the carpark
a man sits behind his wheel.
he is quite still. he has been dead since morning.

Pamela Gillilan

SIMON THIRSK

Selection from: *That Winter* (1986).

PAMELA GILLILAN was born in London, married in 1948 and moved to Cornwall in 1951. When she sat down to write her poem *Come Away* after the death of her husband David, she had written no poetry for a quarter of a century. Then came a sequence of incredibly moving elegies.

Other poems followed: acutely remembered stories of friends and relatives from the past, and reminiscences stretching back to her childhood. Two years after starting to write again, Pamela Gillilan won the Cheltenham Festival poetry competition. In 1987 she was nominated for the Commonwealth Poetry Prize as the UK's best first-time published poet. ●

When You Died

1.

When you died
I went through the rain
Carrying my nightmare
To register the death.

A well-groomed healthy gentleman
Safe within his office
Said – Are you the widow?

Couldn't he have said
Were you his wife?

2.

After the first shock
I found I was
Solidly set in my flesh.
I was an upright central pillar,
The soft flesh melted round me.
My eyes melted
Spilling the inexhaustible essence of sorrow.

The soft flesh of the body
Melted onto chairs and into beds
Dragging its emptiness and pain.

I lodged inside holding myself upright,
Warding off the dreadful deliquescence.

3.

November.
Stooping under muslins
Of grey rain I fingered
Through ribbons of wet grass,
Traced stiff stems down to the wormy earth
And one by one snapped off
The pale surviving flowers; they would ride
With him, lie on the polished plank
Above his breast.

People said – Why do you not
Follow the coffin?
Why do you not
Have any funeral words spoken?
Why not
Send flowers from a shop?

4.

When you died
They burnt you.
They brought home to me
A vase of thin metal;
Inside, a plasty bag
Crammed, full of gritty pieces.
Ground bones, not silky ash.

Where shall I put this substance?
Shall I scatter it
With customary thoughts
Of nature's mystical balance
Among the roses?

Shall I disperse it into the winds
That blow across Cambeake Cliff
Or drop it onto places where you
Lived, worked, were happy?

Finally shall I perhaps keep it
Which after all was you
Quietly on a shelf
And when I follow
My old grit can lie
No matter where with yours
Slowly sinking into the earth together.

5.

When you died
I did not for the moment
Think about myself;
I grieved deeply and purely for your loss,
That you had lost your life.
I grieved bitterly for your mind destroyed,
Your courage thrown away,
Your senses aborted under the amazing skin
No one would ever touch again.

I grieve still
That we'd have grown
Even more deeply close and old together
And now shall not.

Two Years

When you died
All the doors banged shut.

After two years, inch by inch,
They creep open.
Now I can relish
Small encounters,
Encourage
Small flares of desire;

Begin to believe as you did
Things come right.
I tell myself that you
Escaped the slow declension to old age
Leaving me to indulge
This wintry flowering.

But I know
It's not like that at all.

Four Years

The smell of him went soon
From all his shirts.
I sent them for jumble,
And the sweaters and suits.
The shoes
Held more of him; he was printed
Into his shoes. I did not burn
Or throw or give them away.
Time has denatured them now.

Nothing left.
There never will be
A hair of his in a comb.
But I want to believe
That in the shifting housedust
Minute presences still drift:
An eyelash,
A hard crescent cut from a fingernail,
That sometimes
Between the folds of a curtain
Or the covers of a book
I touch
A flake of his skin.

Jenny Joseph

SIMON THIRSK

JENNY JOSEPH was born in 1932 in Birmingham. Her second book of poems, *Rose in the Afternoon* (1974), won her a Cholmondeley Award. Two books followed from Secker: *The Thinking Heart* (1978) and *Beyond Descartes* (1983). Her Bloodaxe *Selected Poems* includes work from all these books.

Persephone, her first work of fiction, won the James Tait Black Memorial Prize. ●

Selection from *Selected Poems* (1991).

Dawn walkers
from SELECTED POEMS

Anxious eyes loom down the damp-black streets
Pale staring girls who are walking away hard
From beds where love went wrong or died or turned away,
Treading their misery beneath another day
Stamping to work into another morning.

In all our youths there must have been some time
When the cold dark has stiffened up the wind
But suddenly, like a sail stiffening with wind,
Carried the vessel on, stretching the ropes, glad of it.

But listen to this now: this I saw one morning.
I saw a young man running, for a bus I thought,
Needing to catch it on this murky morning
Dodging the people crowding to work or shopping early.
And all heads stopped and turned to see how he ran
To see would he make it, the beautiful strong young man.
Then I noticed a girl running after, calling out 'John'.
He must have left his sandwiches I thought.
But she screamed 'John wait'. He heard her and ran faster,
Using his muscled legs and studded boots.
We knew she'd never reach him. 'Listen to me John.
Only once more' she cried. 'For the last time, John, please wait,
    please listen.'

He gained the corner in a spurt and she
Sobbing and hopping with her red hair loose
(Made way for by the respectful audience)
Followed on after, but not to catch him now.
Only that there was nothing left to do.

The street closed in and went on with its day.
A worn old man standing in the heat from the baker's
Said 'Surely to God the bastard could have waited'.

Brendan Kennelly

IAN GROUND

BRENDAN KENNELLY was born in 1936 in Ballylongford, County Kerry, and is now Professor of Modern Literature at Trinity College, Dublin. He has published over 20 books, and edited the *Penguin Book of Irish Verse*.

In Ireland his poetry is rated as highly as Heaney's, and many Irish critics regard Kennelly's *Cromwell* as the most important work in Irish literature since Kavanagh's *Great Hunger*. It is a sequence of nearly 300 poems featuring Oliver Cromwell and a hapless character called Buffún (Kennelly's alter-ego?), who is wracked by the living nightmare of Irish history. It is a masterpiece of poetic imagination: violent, grotesque, comic, and stunning. ●

Selection from: *A Time for Voices* (1990) and *Cromwell* (1987).

The Visitor

from A TIME FOR VOICES

He strutted into the house.

Laughing
He walked over to the woman
Stuck a kiss in her face.

He wore gloves.
He had fur on his coat.
He was the most confident man in the world.
He liked his own wit.

Turning his attention to the children
He patted each one on the head.
They are healthy but a bit shy, he said.
They'll make fine men and women, he said.

The children looked up at him.
He was still laughing.
He was so confident
They could not find the word for it.
He was so elegant
He was more terrifying than the giants of night.

The world
Could only go on its knees before him.
The kissed woman
Was expected to adore him.

It seemed she did.

I'll eat now, he said,
Nothing elaborate, just something simple and quick –
Rashers, eggs, sausages, tomatoes
And a few nice lightly-buttered slices
Of your very own
Home-made brown
Bread.
O you dear woman, can't you see
My tongue is hanging out
For a pot of your delicious tea.
No other woman in this world
Can cook so well for me.

I'm always touched by your modest mastery!

He sat at table like a king.
He ate between bursts of laughter.
He was a great philosopher,
Wise, able to advise,
Solving the world between mouthfuls.
The woman hovered about him.
The children stared at his vital head.
He had robbed them of every word they had.
Please have some more food, the woman said.
He ate, he laughed, he joked,
He knew the world, his plate was clean
As Jack Spratt's in the funny poem,
He was a handsome wolfman,
More gifted than anyone
The woman and children of that house
Had ever seen or known.

He was the storm they listened to at night
Huddled together in bed
He was what laid the woman low
With the killing pain in her head

He was the threat in the high tide
At the back of the house
He was a huge knock on the door
In a moment of peace
He was a hound's neck leaning
Into the kill
He was a hawk of heaven stooping
To fulfil its will
He was the sentence tired writers of gospel
Prayed God to write
He was a black explosion of starlings
Out of a November tree
He was a plan that worked
In a climate of self-delight
He was all the voices
Of the sea.

My time is up, he said,
I must go now.

Taking his coat, gloves, philosophy, laughter, wit,
He prepared to leave.
He kissed the woman again.
He smiled down on the children.
He walked out of the house.
The children looked at each other.
The woman looked at the chair.
The chair was a throne
Bereft of its king, its visitor.

A Glimpse of Starlings
from A TIME FOR VOICES

I expect him any minute now although
He's dead. I know he has been talking
All night to his own dead and now
In the first heart-breaking light of morning
He is struggling into his clothes,
Sipping a cup of tea, fingering a bit of bread,
Eating a small photograph with his eyes.

The questions bang and rattle in his head
Like doors and cannisters the night of a storm.
He doesn't know why his days finished like this
Daylight is as hard to swallow as food
Love is a crumb all of him hungers for.
I can hear the drag of his feet on the concrete path
The close explosion of his smoker's cough
The slow turn of the Yale key in the lock
The door opening to let him in
To what looks like release from what feels like pain
And over his shoulder a glimpse of starlings
Suddenly lifted over field, road and river
Like a fist of black dust pitched in the wind.

Manager, Perhaps?
from CROMWELL

The first time I met Oliver Cromwell
The poor man was visibly distressed.
'Buffún' says he, 'things are gone to the devil
In England. So I popped over here for a rest.
Say what you will about Ireland, where on
Earth could a harassed statesman find peace like
This in green unperturbed oblivion?
Good Lord! I'm worn out from intrigue and work.
I'd like a little estate down in Kerry,
A spot of salmon-fishing, riding to hounds.
Good Lord! The very thought makes me delighted.
Being a sporting chap, I'd really love to
Get behind one of the best sides in the land.
Manager, perhaps, of Drogheda United?'

Nails
from CROMWELL

The black van exploded
Fifty yards from the hotel entrance.
Two men, one black-haired, the other red,
Had parked it there as though for a few moments
While they walked around the corner
Not noticing, it seemed, the children

In single file behind their perky leader,
And certainly not seeing the van
Explode into the children's bodies.
Nails, nine inches long, lodged
In chest, ankle, thigh, buttock, shoulder, face.
The quickly-gathered crowd was outraged and shocked.
Some children were whole, others bits and pieces.
These blasted crucifixions are commonplace.

Stewart Conn

Selection from: *In the Kibble Palace: new & selected poems* (1987).

STEWART CONN was born in 1936 in Glasgow, and grew up in Ayrshire. He now lives in Edinburgh, where he works as a BBC radio drama producer. He is one of Scotland's finest poets.

His early poems draw on memories of his farming background, the people looming larger than life in stories of their near heroic deeds – as seen through the child's (or poet's) eye. 'They become figures in a private mythology,' Dannie Abse has written, 'they are figures caught up heroically in elemental violence' (as in the poem *Ferret*). Of his later poetry, Robert Nye has said: 'Conn frets away at dark states of mind and the heart's unease in terms of landscape patched with shadow.' ●

Visiting Hour

In the pond of our new garden
were five orange stains, under
inches of ice. Weeks since anyone
had been there. Already by far
the most severe winter for years.
You broke the ice with a hammer.
I watched the goldfish appear,
blunt-nosed and delicately clear.

Since then so much has taken place
to distance us from what we were.
That it should come to this.
Unable to hide the horror
in my eyes, I stand helpless
by your bedside and can do no more
than wish it were simply a matter
of smashing the ice and giving you air.

C.K. Williams

CATHERINE MAUGER

Selection from: *Poems 1963-1983* (1988).

C.K. WILLIAMS was born in 1936 in Newark, New Jersey, and now lives in Paris. He is the most challenging American poet of his generation, a poet of intense and searching originality who makes lyric sense out of the often brutal realities of everyday life. Stanley Kunitz calls him 'a wonderful poet in the authentic American tradition of Whitman and W.C. Williams, who tells us on every page what it means to be alive in our time.'

His *Poems 1963-1983* draws on his first four books. His latest collection, *Flesh and Blood*, won America's prestigious National Book Critics Circle poetry award. Both books are published by Farrar, Straus & Giroux in America and by Bloodaxe in Britain. ●

Neglect

An old hill town in northern Pennsylvania, a missed connection for a
    bus, an hour to kill.
For all intents and purposes, the place was uninhabited; the mines
    had closed years before –
anthracite too dear to dig, the companies went west to strip, the
    miners to the cities –
and now, although the four-lane truck route still went through –
    eighteen-wheelers pounding past –
that was almost all: a shuttered Buick dealer, a grocery, not even a
    McDonald's,
just the combination ticket office, luncheonette, and five-and-dime
    where the buses turned around.
A low, gray frame building, it was gloomy and rundown, but charmingly
    old-fashioned:
ancient wooden floors, open shelves, the smell of unwrapped candy,
    cigarettes and band-aid glue.
The only people there, the only people I think that I remember from
    the town at all,
were the silent woman at the register and a youngish teen-aged boy
    standing reading.
The woman smoked and smoked, stared out the streaky window,
    handed me my coffee with indifference.

It was hard to tell how old she was: her hair was dyed and teased,
iced into a beehive.
The boy was frail, sidelong somehow, afflicted with a devastating
Nessus-shirt of acne
boiling down his face and neck – pits and pores, scarlet streaks and
scars; saddening.
We stood together at the magazine rack for a while before I realised
what he was looking at.
Pornography: two naked men, one grimaces, the other, with a fist
inside the first one, grins.
I must have flinched: the boy sidled down, blanked his face once
more and I left to take a walk.
It was cold, but not enough to catch or clear your breath: uncertain
clouds, unemphatic light.
Everything seemed dimmed and colorless, the sense of surfaces
dissolving, like the Parthenon.
Farther down the main street were a dentist and a chiropractor,
both with hand-carved signs,
then the Elks' decaying clapboard mansion with a parking space
'Reserved for the Exalted Ruler',
and a Russian church, gilt onion domes, a four-horned air-raid
siren on a pole between them.
Two blocks in, the old slate sidewalks shatter and uplift – gnawed
lawns, aluminium butane tanks –
then the roads begin to peter out and rise: half-fenced yards with
scabs of weeks-old snow,
thin, inky, oily leaks of melt insinuating down the gulleys and the
cindered cuts
that rose again into the footings of the filthy, disused slagheaps
ringing the horizon.
There was nowhere else. At the depot now, the woman and the boy
were both behind the counter.
He was on a stool, his eyes closed, she stood just in back of him,
massaging him,
hauling at his shoulders, kneading at the muscles like a boxer's trainer
between rounds.
I picked up the county paper: it was anti-crime and welfare bums,
for Reaganomics and defense.
The wire-photo was an actress in her swimming suit, that famously
expensive bosom, cream.
My bus arrived at last, its heavy, healthy white exhaust pouring in
the afternoon.

Glancing back, I felt a qualm, concern, an ill heart, almost parental,
    but before I'd hit the step,
the boy'd begun to blur, to look like someone else, the woman had
    already faded absolutely.
All that held now was that violated, looted country, the fraying fringes
    of the town,
those gutted hills, hills by rote, hills by permission, great, naked
    wastes of wrack and spill,
vivid and disconsolate, like genitalia shaved and disinfected for an
    operation.

Sylvia Kantaris

TRACY O'KATES

SYLVIA KANTARIS was born in 1936 in Derbyshire, lived in Australia for some years, and now lives in Cornwall. 'Her work is powerful, sensual, passionate and controlled' (*British Book News*). Her *Dirty Washing* draws on four previous books, including *The Tenth Muse* (1983), *The Sea at the Door* (1985) and *News from the Front*, a collaboration with D.M. Thomas. ●

Selection from: *Dirty Washing: new & selected poems* (1989).

Windy Monday

The wind billows like a stuffed shirt this washday.
I spin the man and peg him on my line to bloat and puff out
with the full authority of wind, like bladderwrack.

It is a pumped-up Dunlopillo president of no parts,
portly with nothingness, his flap a clackety-clack
of digits at the laundromat. O windy diplomat,

keeping up your sleeve an aftershave of sundry secrets
like a Company Director of the Stock Exchange,
your pockets stuffed with wads of air like multiple zeros.

Magnate of the wrangled fleet of sheets and honourable
Fellow of the Faithful Flock of Pillowslips,
you lord it in full sail of pomp and circumstance.

Our man of wind is tested by the whiteness test
of God's own cleanliness and rinsed in *Comfort* –
a full-blown representative of earthly windbags.

In consequence whereof (and so forth) drizzle is undiplomatic.
It winds him. Now he sags and blusters, breathless.
I am not sad to see him shrink like that,

cuddling his own flatness in his flattened arms, like flatness,
or a little flag of little consequence,
soggy with such sadness like a dishrag.

I'll leave him there all night to hang and ghost it
in the moonlight and get bleached (whiter than white).
Why should I let a Man of Consequence drip dry like cuckoo-spit
        on my hearth?

Matt Simpson

HARRY NOVAK

Selection from: *Making Arrangements* (1982).

MATT SIMPSON was born in 1936 in Bootle, and in many of his poems looks back at his upbringing there, at family tensions in a close-knit Merseyside community with strong seafaring traditions, as in the two poems here.

'What Simpson gives us is something entirely his own, a unified dockland reverie that interweaves family history, an elliptical narrative of childhood and adolescence in a sharply realised place and time, war, street wisdoms and the trades of the sea. It's done by anecdote, by portrait, by quizzical meditation...and more than anything else, by elegy' – Kit Wright. ●

My Grandmother's African Grey

My father's brother brought it home,
madcap Cliff, a 'case', with wit as wild
as erotic dreams. It was his proof
of Africa and emblem of the family pride
in seamanship.
                    But the parrot quickly sensed
our pride was ragged. Perverse, it
nipped its feathers out
with tar-black pincering beak, until,
baring a stubbly breast, it looked
like poultry obscenely undead.

A gift to grandma and to Auntie Bell
who lived together, two odd shoes
inside a wardrobe of a house, it learnt
to parody my grandma's Liverpudlian
wash-house talk, her lovely common-
as-muck, which it counterpointed faithfully
with Auntie Bell's posh how-d'you-do's
that froze you to politeness:
Sunday Best, with little finger cocked.

The bird survived them both, lost all sense
of Africa, one quarter of a century on a perch.
Shabby slate-grey feathers came to mean
my grandmother; its tail's red splash
was Auntie Bell – their stout and brandy accents
jangling on inside the cage.

Homecoming

Due on the tide, my father's rusted hulk,
weary from landings at Sicily, sailed
into blitzed Liverpool under the waving swords
of searchlights, into the flash and batter of
the ack-ack guns. Under a sky in panic,
into the erupting port, up-river he came
urging home his helpless and unspeaking love.

Next morning, docked, he slung his canvas bag
about his shoulders like a drunken mate, himself
unsteady in the smoking, settling air, and walked
into our street, turning the corner by
the foundry. The street was flattened – brick and wood
in scorched disorder. 'I thought that you were goners,'
he afterwards said, finding us safe up-town
at my grandma's house.

And I remember the last few days,
the quivering run-up hours to that street's death:
a five-year-old and his mother hunched
under the stairs, with the fat chrome springs
of an obsolete pram jigging over my head
and plaster puffing white dust in our hair,
the sky droning and tingling blasts
as a neighbouring street went down.

'We moved that day,' my mother used to say,
'and that same night your dad came home.'
She prized the weird coincidence. It was
as if someone had given her flowers.

Ken Smith

MOIRA CONWAY

KEN SMITH was born in 1938 in Rudston, the son of a farm labourer. He grew up in rural Yorkshire, was uprooted to Hull, spent some years in America, and now lives in London.

His Bloodaxe titles are *Burned Books* (1981), *The Poet Reclining: Selected Poems 1962-1980* (1982), *Terra* (1986), *Wormwood* (1987), *A Book of Chinese Whispers* (1987), his collected prose, and *The heart, the border* (1990) ●

Selection from: *The Poet Reclining: Selected Poems 1962-1980* (1982) and *Terra* (1986).

Family Group

He also was a stormy day: a squat mountain man
smelling of sheep and the high pasture, stumping
through pinewoods, hunched and small, feeling
the weather on him. Work angled him.
Fingers were crooked with frost, stiffened.

Ploughing he would fix his eye on the hawthorn,
walking firm-booted, concerned for the furrow.
Horse and man in motion together, deliberate,
one foot put before the other, treading cut clay.
He would not see the bird perched on the plough.
He would not chase the plover limping over stubble.

He was my father who brought in wood and lit
the hissing lamp. And he would sit, quiet
as moor before the fire. She drew him
slowly out of silence. She had a coat
made from a blanket and wore boys' shoes.
She was small and had red hands, firm-boned,
and her hair was greying. The house was stone
and slate. It was her house, his home,
and their family, and they quarrelled often.

She churned butter, baked, and scrubbed floors,
and for forty years he laboured the raw earth
and rough weather. In winter we made mats
from rags with pegs. We guarded ourselves
and were close. We were poor and poorer banking
each pound saved. Each year passed slowly.

Now he lives in the glass world of his shop,
and time is grudged. Ham and tinned meat
and vegetables are his breathing day.
He works harder and is unhappy. She too
stoops through the labouring year, is greyer
and grumbles. Nothing gets made any more
but money that cannot be made. Nothing
means happiness. The light comes down wires,
water through tubes. All is expensive, paid.

Silence is gone from their lives, the city
has taken that poised energy. Violence
is articulate. The deliberate motion is gone
and he moves with pain through time that is work
that is cash. He will not notice the crashed
gull fallen in the storm, the grabbing sparrows.
She cannot ease him into speech, or be content
before the broody fire. She is in fashion now.
But seasons pass them without touching.
They will not feel the winter when it comes.

Bogart in the dumb waiter
after Dashiell Hammett
from TERRA

This is genuine coin of the realm.
A dollar of this buys ten of talk.
The cheaper the crook the gaudier the patter.
I'll see you at the inquest maybe.

I'm a reasonable man. I don't mind
a reasonable amount of trouble.
All I've got to do is stand still
and they'll be swarming all over me.

More than idle curiosity prompts my question:
how'd you like to turn my chops over?
Yes. I'm tired of lying, tired of lies,
of not knowing what the truth is.

So listen carefully here's the plot:
the grieving widow walks on, grieves,
walks off again still grieving.
You want to hang around you'll be polite.

You get loose teeth talking like that.
You're taking the fall, precious.
If you're a good girl they'll give you life.
If they hang you I'll always remember you.

The shortest farewell's best: adieu.
Here's to plain speaking and clear understanding.
I distrust a close mouthed man. I'm a man
who likes talking to a man who likes to talk.

Frances Horovitz

MIKE GOLDING

Selection from: *Collected Poems* (1985), edited by Roger Garfitt.

FRANCES HOROVITZ was born in 1938 in London. Many of her poems were inspired by the remote Cotswold valley where she lived for ten years; others by the border country of Cumbria and the Welsh Marches. The poems here, from *Snow Light, Water Light* (1983), came out of two winters spent in a farmhouse on Hadrian's Wall – near the Roman fort of Birdoswald, and Camboglanna (or the Crooked Glen), reputed site of Arthur's last battle. She died in 1983, after a long illness. 'Evening' was one of the last poems she wrote.

'She has perfect rhythm, great delicacy and a rather Chinese yet very locally British sense of landscape... her poetry does seem to me to approach greatness' – Peter Levi. ●

Rain — Birdoswald

I stand under a leafless tree
more still, in this mouse-pattering
    thrum of rain,
than cattle shifting in the field.
    It is more dark than light.
A Chinese painter's brush of deepening grey
    moves in a subtle tide.

The beasts are darker islands now.
Wet-stained and silvered by the rain
    they suffer night,
marooned as still as stone or tree.
    We sense each other's quiet.

Almost, death could come
inevitable, unstrange
    as is this dusk and rain,
and I should be no more
    myself, than raindrops
glimmering in last light
    on black ash buds

or night beasts in a winter field.

Sightings

Flake on flake, snow
packed light as ash
                    or feather,
shavings of crystal.
      By moonlight
stars pulse underfoot.

      The burning fox ran here,
his narrow print
      under gate
                  and over wall
diagonal across the field;
      skeining of rabbit tracks,
our own slurred trail.

      Like black stones
crows squat, sunning
      among staring sheep
– crow's wing
      brushed on snow,
three strokes
      twice etched
as faint and fine
      as fossil bone.

Evening

            Lilac blossom crests the window sill
mingling whiteness with the good dark of this room.
A bloom of light hangs delicately in white painted angles.
Bluebells heaped in a pot
still hold their blue against the dark;
I see their green stalks glisten.

Thin as a swan's bone
I wait for the lessons of pain and light.
Grief is a burden, useless.
It must dissolve into the dark.
I see the hills, luminous.
There will be the holly tree
the hawthorn with mistletoe
foxgloves springing in thousands.

The hills also will pass away
                will remain
as this lilac light, these bluebells,
the good dark of this room.

John Drew

Selection from: *The Lesser Vehicle* (1986).

JOHN DREW was born in 1939 in Kent. As a Fleet Street journalist, he ghosted the William Hickey column for a time. He later spent some years writing a book about how the most imaginative English approaches to India have been by way of Hellenism, *India and the Romantic Imagination* (OUP, 1986), while working as a postman and mail porter at Cambridge railway station. He is now a lecturer in English at Shanghai University.

His first collection *The Lesser Vehicle* was widely praised for its zany, zen-like blend of humour and philosophy: 'Good-humoured but terse bits of mysticism,' said Peter Porter in the *Observer*. 'Drew keeps his feet on the ground while levitating.' ●

Negative Capability

It could not have been
A nightingale, they said.
They said it was a blackbird
Or a thrush that I had seen

Singing above the streetlight
As Christmas Eve closed in.
Call it what they like
I heard its song all night,

No other soul was near me.
If I could sing like that
I should not need a name.
Nor anyone to hear me.

Pauline Stainer

DAVID HUNTER

Selection from: *The Honeycomb* (1989).

PAULINE STAINER was born in 1941, and lives in Dunmow, Essex. She won first prize in the Stroud Festival poetry competition in 1984.

'Her poems are unlike anyone else's, but they're so strong and clear that they bring to mind that in-her-own-time ignored, painfully sensitive yet tough-minded American Metaphysical, Emily Dickinson. Stainer, though, is deeply English and draws from a wealth of sources: medieval lyrics, Eastern as well as Western art, Christian liturgy, and an impressive familiarity with chemistry and optics. But the subjects which engage her are always human, however referentially sacred or scientifically demonstrated' – Anne Stevenson. ●

The Figurehead

He came upon her strangely,
Whilst driving through night-mist:
A ship's figurehead under apple trees
Where the village forked.

The slant-moon
Touched her breasts with spindrift,
Bleached hair
Swept back from her brow;

Her nakedness
So eerily illumined in the orchard,
He saw nothing,
Driving till dawn,

But her beached body,
And through her eyes
With their unchiselled pupils,
The bitter cresses blowing in ghost-ports.

Walking the Water

Feet skirr the membrane –
the child before birth
walking the water.

Siphon from the sac;
amniosis
is ghost on a glass-slide.

X-ray the running-light;
the lit watermark
of the flesh.

Divine
the foetal heartbeat,
the pulse through the caul.

Corpuscles are cautionary magic;
crucifixion
a red suspension in the blood;

visitation
a velvet-runner –
the spirit sexed.

Jeni Couzyn

JENI COUZYN was born in 1942 in South Africa, and grew up in Johannesburg. She emigrated to Britain in 1965, and now lives in London. She edited the *Bloodaxe Book of Contemporary Women Poets* (1985). Her collections include *Flying, Monkeys' Wedding, House of Changes*, and *Christmas in Africa* – with its bittersweet evocations of her African childhood, as in the poem below.

Her Selected Poems, *Life by Drowning*, includes work from all those books, as well as two new sequences, *A Time To Be Born* and *The Coming of the Angel*, containing her most imaginative and spiritually profound poetry. ●

Selection from: *Life by Drowning: Selected Poems* (1985).

From Christmas in Africa

One autumn afternoon when I was nine
feeding the chickens near the grapevine, brooding
in sunshine, my mother asked me to choose

a christmas present that year.
Anything I said, but a doll. Whatever you choose
but not a doll

my faith in her to know
better than I could myself what gift would please me.
And so at the height of summer

we made our pilgrimage
to the earth's greenest riches and the ample ocean.
And christmas eve

was three white daughters
three bright angels singing silent night as my mother
lit the candles

the tree blooming
sea breathing, the beloved son in his cradle sleeping.
Over the hills and skies

on his sleigh the father
the awaited one, made his visitation. Weeks of dreaming
and wondering now

in a box in my hand.
Shoebox size. Not waterwings then or a time machine no
something the size

of a pair of shoes.
Not a pony then or a river canoe. Not a new dress no.
I pulled at the bright bowed ribbons

and little christmas angels
with trembling hands. Underneath the monkey-apple branch
dressed up in baubles and tinsel

and blobs of cotton wool
the sea soaring, stars and the fairy at the treetop
shining

his hand on my shoulder
my mother's eyes on my face two burning suns
piercing my mind and in the box

a doll.
A stupid pretty empty thing. Pink smiling girl. The world
rocked about my head

my face fell into a net
from that moment. My heart in me played possum
and never recovered.

I said I liked the wretched thing
joy broke over my face like a mirror cracking. I said it
so loud, so often

I almost believed it. All that christmas
a shameful secret bound me and the doll and my mother
irrevocably together.

When I knew she was watching
I would grab for the doll in the night, or take it
tenderly with me to the beach

wrapped in a small towel.
At last on the last night of the journey home
staying at a hotel

my mother woke me early
to go out and find the maid. In my pyjamas, half asleep
I staggered out into the dawn

heat rising like mist
from the ground, birds making an uproar, snakes
not yet awake

a sense of something
about to happen under the heavy damp rustle
of the trees.

My feet left footprints
in the dew. When I returned I was clutching that precious
corpse to my chest

like one of the bereaved.
*Now I know, said my mother, that although you didn't
want a doll, you really do love her.*

I was believed!
Something fell from my face with a clatter –
my punishment was over

and in that moment
fell from my mother's face a particular smile, a kind of
dear and tender curling of the eyes

fell. Two gripped faces
side by side on the floor, smiled at each other
before we grabbed them back

and fitted them with a hollow rattle
to our love. And I laid the doll down in a suitcase
and slammed the lid on its face

and never looked at it again.
And in a sense my mother did the same, and in a sense
my punishment and hers

had always been, and just begun.

Eiléan Ní Chuilleanáin

EILÉAN NÍ CHUILLEANÁIN was born in 1942 in Cork, and now lives in Dublin, where she teaches at Trinity College and co-edits the literary magazine Cyphers. Her Selected Poems, *The Second Voyage*, is published in Ireland by Gallery and in Britain by Bloodaxe. It is a selection from three previous award-winning books, *Acts and Monuments*, *Site of Ambush*, and *The Rose-Geranium*. Her other books include *Cork* (1977) and *Irish Women: Image and Achievement* (1985).

'Eiléan Ní Chuilleanáin's dreamlike work is haunting, alien, full of awe' – *Eire-Ireland*. ●

Selection from: *The Second Voyage* (1986).

The House Remembered

The house persists, the permanent
Scaffolding while the stones move round.
Convolvulus winds the bannisters, sucks them down;
We found an icicle under the stairs
Tall as a church candle;
It refused to answer questions
But proved its point by freezing hard.

The house changes, the stones
Choking in dry lichen stupidly spreading
Abusing the doorposts, frost on the glass.
Nothing stays still, the house is still the same
But the breast over the sink turned into a tap
And coming through the door all fathers look the same.

The stairs and windows waver but the house stands up;
Peeling away the walls another set shows through.
I can't remember, it all happened too recently.
But somebody was born in every room.

Deaths and Engines

We came down above the houses
In a stiff curve, and
At the edge of Paris airport
Saw an empty tunnel
– The back half of a plane, black
On the snow, nobody near it,
Tubular, burnt-out and frozen.

When we faced again
The snow-white runways in the dark
No sound came over
The loudspeakers, except the sighs
Of the lonely pilot.

The cold of metal wings is contagious:
Soon you will need wings of your own,
Cornered in the angle where
Time and life like a knife and fork
Cross, and the lifeline in your palm
Breaks, and the curve of an aeroplane's track
Meets the straight skyline.

The images of relief:
Hospital pyjamas, screens round a bed
A man with a bloody face
Sitting up in bed, conversing cheerfully
Through cut lips:
These will fail you some time.

You will find yourself alone
Accelerating down a blind
Alley, too late to stop
And know how light your death is;
You will be scattered like wreckage,
The pieces every one a different shape
Will spin and lodge in the hearts
Of all who love you.

David Constantine

DAVID CONSTANTINE was born in 1944 in Sal-
ford, Lancashire. He is a lecturer in German
at Oxford. As well as three books of poems,
he has published a novel, *Davies* (1985), with
Bloodaxe. His second collection, *Watching
for Dolphins*, won the Alice Hunt Bartlett
Prize in 1984; his third *Madder*, is a Poetry
Book Society Recommendation. His *Selected
Poems* of Friedrich Hölderlin was published
by Bloodaxe in 1990. ●

Selection from: *Watching
for Dolphins* (1983).

Watching for Dolphins

In the summer months on every crossing to Piraeus
One noticed that certain passengers soon rose
From seats in the packed saloon and with serious
Looks and no acknowledgement of a common purpose
Passed forward through the small door into the bows
To watch for dolphins. One saw them lose

Every other wish. Even the lovers
Turned their desires on the sea, and a fat man
Hung with equipment to photograph the occasion
Stared like a saint, through sad bi-focals; others,
Hopeless themselves, looked to the children for they
Would see dolphins if anyone would. Day after day

Or on their last opportunity all gazed
Undecided whether a flat calm were favourable
Or a sea the sun and the wind between them raised
To a likeness of dolphins. Were gulls a sign, that fell
Screeching from the sky or over an unremarkable place
Sat in a silent school? Every face

After its character implored the sea.
All, unaccustomed, wanted epiphany,
Praying the sky would clang and the abused Aegean
Reverberate with cymbal, gong and drum.

We could not imagine more prayer, and had they then
On the waves, on the climax of our longing come

Smiling, snub-nosed, domed like satyrs, oh
We should have laughed and lifted the children up
Stranger to stranger, pointing how with a leap
They left their element, three or four times, centred
On grace, and heavily and warm re-entered,
Looping the keel. We should have felt them go

Further and further into the deep parts. But soon
We were among the great tankers, under their chains
In black water. We had not seen the dolphins
But woke, blinking. Eyes cast down
With no admission of disappointment the company
Dispersed and prepared to land in the city.

'Pity the drunks'

Pity the drunks in this late April snow.
They drank their hats and coats a week ago.
They touched the sun, they tapped the melting ground,
In public parks we saw them sitting round
The merry campfire of a cider jar
Upon a crocus cloth. Alas, some are
Already stiff in mortuaries who were
Seduced by Spring to go from here to there,
Putting their best foot forward on the road
To Walkden, Camberwell or Leeds. It snowed.
It met them waiting at the roundabout.
They had no hats and coats to keep it out.
They did a lap or two, they caught a cough.
They did another lap and shuffled off.

Peter Didsbury

PAT DIDSBURY

PETER DIDSBURY was born in 1946 in Fleetwood, Lancashire, and moved to Hull at the age of six. He taught English at a large Hull comprehensive for eight years, and is now a medieval pottery researcher. When his first book *The Butchers of Hull* appeared, the *Times Literary Supplement* called him 'the best new poet that the excellent Bloodaxe Books have yet published'. His second collection, *The Classical Farm*, is a Poetry Book Society Recommendation.

Selection from: *The Butchers of Hull* (1982) and *The Classical Farm* (1987).

'Some of his invention is pure play, some hints darkly at a rich humane vision of England...oblique, desperate celebrations... gallows irony, eccentric erudition...an arresting, highly individual voice' – Alan Jenkins, *The Observer*. ●

The Drainage
from THE BUTCHERS OF HULL

When he got out of bed the world had changed.
It was very cold. His breath whitened the room.
Chill December clanked at the panes.
There was freezing fog.
He stepped outside.
Not into his street but a flat wet landscape.
Sluices. Ditches. Drains. Frozen mud and leafcake. Dykes.
He found he knew the names of them all.
Barber's Cut. Cold Track. Lament. Meridian Stream.
He found himself walking.
It was broad cold day but the sky was black.
Instead of the sun it was Orion there.
Seeming to pulse his meaning down.
He was naked. He had to clothe himself.
The heifers stood like statues in the fields.
They didn't moan when he sliced the hides from them.
He looked at the penknife in his hand.
The needle, the thread, the clammy strips.
Now his face mooned out through a white hole.
The cape dripped. He knew he had
the bounds of a large parish to go.
His feet refused to falter.

Birds sat still in the trees.
Fast with cold glue. Passing their clumps
he watched them rise in their species.
The individuals. Sparrow. Starling. Wren.
He brought them down with his finger.
Knife needle and thread again.
It happened with the streams.
Pike barbel roach minnow gudgeon.
Perch dace eel. Grayling lamprey bream.
His feet cracked puddles and were cut on mud. They bled.
There was movement. He pointed. He stitched.
His coat hung reeking on him.
He made cut after cut in the cold.
Coldness and the colours of blood.
Red blue and green. He glistened.
He stitched through white fat.
Weight of pelts and heads. Nodding at the hem.
Feathers. Scales. Beaks and strips of skin.
He had the bounds of a large parish to go.
Oh Christ, he moaned. Sweet Christ.
The Hunter hung stretched in the Sky.
He looked at the creatures of the bankside.
He glistened. He pointed. He stitched.

In Britain
from THE BUTCHERS OF HULL

The music, on fat bellied instruments.
The fingers, swarming down ladders
into the bubbling cauldrons of sound.
The mouths, greasy, encouraging the prying fingers
with songs of fecund stomachs.
The hands, transferring to the singing mouths
whatever is lifted through the scum.
The choicest morsels, the collops of dog and the
gobbets of pig. The orchestras and bands,
the minstrelsy arranged in tiers,
dripping on each other. The larded steps.
The treacherous floors in the wooden galleries.
The garlands of offal, plopping on heads
from a height of some feet.

The offal sliding off down the front of the face,
or over the neck and ears. The offal reposing like hats.
The curly grey-white tubes, dangling jauntily
above the left eye of the bagpipe player.
The guests, similarly festooned.
The guests at their conversation,
abundance of dogs and pigs in these islands.
The guests at their serious business, lying in pools.
The stories, farting and belching across the puddled boards.
The gross imaginations, bulging with viscera.
The heads full of stories, the stories thwacked like bladders.
The stories steaming in time to the music.
The stories, chewed like lumps of gristle.
The stories describing extravagant herds.
The stories, reasons for killing each other.

The Hailstone

Standing under the greengrocer's awning
in the kind of rain we used to call a cloudburst,
getting home later with a single hailstone in my hair.
Ambition would have us die in thunderstorms
like Jung and Mahler. Five minutes now,
for all our sad and elemental loves.

A woman sheltering inside the shop
had a frightened dog,
which she didn't want us to touch.
It had something to do with class,
and the ownership of fear. Broken ceramic lightning
was ripping open the stitching in the sky.
The rain was "siling" down,
the kind that comes bouncing back off the pavement,
heavy milk from the ancient skins
being poured through the primitive strainer.
Someone could have done us in flat colours,
formal and observant, all on one plane,
you and me outside and the grocer and the lady
behind the gunmetal glass, gazing out over our shoulders.

I can see the weave of the paper behind the smeared reflections,
some of the colour lifting as we started a sudden dash home.
We ran by the post office and I thought, 'It is all still true,
a wooden drawer is full of postal orders, it is raining,
mothers and children are standing in their windows,
I am running through the rain past a shop which sells wool,
you take home fruit and veg in bags of brown paper,
we are getting wet, it is raining.'
                                        It was like being back
in the reign of George the Sixth, the kind of small town
which still lies stacked in the back of old storerooms in schools,
where plural roof and elf expect to get very wet
and the beasts deserve their nouns of congregation
as much as the postmistress, spinster, her title.
I imagine those boroughs as intimate with rain,
their ability to call on sentient functional downpours
for any picnic or trip to the German Butcher's
one sign of a usable language getting used,
make of this what you will. The rain has moved on,
and half a moon in a darkening blue sky
silvers the shrinking puddles in the road:
moon that emptied the post office and grocer's,
moon old kettle of rain and idiolect,
the moon the sump of the aproned pluvial towns,
cut moon as half a hailstone in the hair.

Paul Hyland

GEORGE TUCKER

PAUL HYLAND was born in 1947 in Dorset. He is a freelance writer specialising in topography and travel, and has published books on the Isle of Wight and Isle of Purbeck. *The Black Heart*, published by Gollancz in 1988, follows a journey he made up the Zaire River in Africa in 1985, retracing the steps of his explorer uncle, Dan Crawford.

His poetry books include *The Stubborn Forest*, which draws on the landscapes of Dorset and other parts of South West England, and his fictional *Poems of Z*, the work of an Eastern Bloc spy who operated in London. 'Z' fled the country, leaving behind a notebook of 40 poems, written in English. ●

Selection from: *The Stubborn Forest* (1984).

Farrier's Dog

Here's one dog won't get under horse's hoofs;
he sits, haunched-up attention, by the forge,
belly like bellows and tooth-printed tongue.

His master heats and hammers soft pink iron,
chimes nail-holes through; dog blinks through parted air;
horse flicks its flank, sweats, lights a livid eye.

The man slaps its taut neck, hefts up its foot
against his thigh and with a quick knife pares
hoof-rind away; the dog whines silently.

The red shoe is by burning bedded in;
from out a thick gout of ammonia smoke
and thin steam spurting when the shoe is quenched

a mess of parings comes, kicked to the dog
who in crouched, greedy spasms gulps it down;
iron is hammered home, and the horse stamps.

Douglas Houston

MOIRA CONWAY

Selection from: *With the Offal Eaters* (1986).

DOUGLAS HOUSTON was born in 1947 in Cardiff, and grew up in Scotland. After 15 years in Hull, he moved back to Wales in 1982, and now lives near Aberystwyth. When his poems appeared in Douglas Dunn's Hull anthology *A Rumoured City*, the *Observer*'s poetry critic Peter Porter relished their 'exaltation of strangeness' and *London Magazine*'s Herbert Lomas savoured his 'images of comic fanciful beauty'.

His first collection, *With the Offal Eaters*, won a Welsh Arts Council Book Award in 1987. 'Quite the most entertaining volume of poems I've read this year and probably the most original' – John Lucas, *New Statesman*. ●

To the Management

I have used your buses for eighteen years.
The day after the new rubber bands came
It occurred to me to write to you.
I was examining an orange pippin
Beneath my desk lamp. Flecks of red
Like dabs of bird's blood grew dense on one side,
The other bald and green. A wonderful sight.
Why not fix small lamps on the seat backs
For people to examine their fruit carefully?
Wash-hand basins should be provided;
Some who use your services are not clean.
I enclose my design which incorporates
A pillar box and cigarette machine.
Your buses should stop outside our houses;
Most of us live on roads of some sort.
A change of colour would be welcome.
Margaret and I thought a shade of lilac.
Personally, I'd appreciate some facility
For heating the tea-cosy I wear on my head,
Which could certainly be put to other uses.

David Scott

MOIRA CONWAY

Selection from: *A Quiet Gathering* (1984) and *Playing for England* (1989).

DAVID SCOTT was born in 1947 in Cambridge. Since 1980 he has been the vicar of Torpenhow and Allhallows near Wigton in Cumbria. He won the *Sunday Times*/BBC national poetry competition in 1978 with the poem *Kirkwall Auction Mart*. His first book of poems, *A Quiet Gathering*, won the Geoffrey Faber Memorial Prize in 1986.

'Scott belongs firmly to the long tradition of parson-poets that goes back to George Herbert... For all their reticence, there is a compassion in these poems and a sense of propriety' – Norman Nicholson, *Church Times*. 'Immaculate poems... full of gentle, contemplative intelligence and a tenacious modesty... scrupulous, affectionate' – John Mole, *Encounter*. ●

Flanking Sheep in Mosedale
from A QUIET GATHERING

All summer the sheep were strewn like crumbs
across the fell, until the bracken turned brittle
and it was time they were gathered
into the green patchwork of closer fields.
Dogs and men sweep a whole hillside in minutes
save for the stray, scared into a scramble
up a gully. A dog is detached: whistled off
by the shepherd who in one hand
holds a pup straining at the baling twine
and in the other, a crook light as a baton.
His call cuts the wind across the tarn:
it is the voice of the first man, who
booted it across this patch to bring
strays to the place where he would have them.
You can tell that here is neither love nor money
but the old game fathers have taught sons to win.
It is done well, when the dogs
lie panting, and the sheep encircled dare not move.

The Surplice
from PLAYING FOR ENGLAND

To think so many battles have been fought
over this four and a half yard circumference
of white linen. Not just by those who ironed it
up to the difficult tucks beneath the yoke
but by Divines wrangling over rubrics.
For me it is my only finery, by law
decent and comely; a vestry friend
put on often in dread; given away
to old deft fingers to mend.
I have seen them hanging in as many ways
as there have been voices chanting in them:
immaculate in hanging wardrobes; or worn
with the peg mark still obtruding;
or chucked on the back seat of the car
with the purple stole and the shopping.
We have put these garments on for centuries.
They persist. We wither and crease inside them.

Locking the Church
from PLAYING FOR ENGLAND

It takes two hands to turn the key
of the church door, and on its stiffest days
needs a piece of iron to work it like a capstan.
I know the key's weight in the hand
the day begins and ends with it.
Tonight the sky is wide open
and locking the church is a walk
between the yews and a field of stars.
The moon is the one I have known
on those first nights away from home.
It dodges behind the bell-cote
and then appears as punched putty or a coin.
The key has a nail for the night
behind the snecked front door.

Carrying a tray of waters up to bed
I halt a careful tread to squint
through curtains not quite met
at the church, the moon, and the silver light
cast on the upturned breasts of the parish dead
locked out for the night.

Ciarán Carson

GALLERY PRESS

Selection from: *The Irish for No* (1988).

CIARÁN CARSON was born in 1948 in Belfast. He is a musician and works as Traditional Arts Officer for the Arts Council of Northern Ireland; his *Pocket Guide to Irish Traditional Music* appeared in 1986.

He won a Gregory Award for his first collection, *The New Estate*. His second, *The Irish for No*, is published by Gallery in Ireland and Bloodaxe in Britain: 'The most remarkable collection by an Irish poet in a year which gave us important new collections by such as Heaney, Muldoon and Kinsella. Carson's subject is Belfast past and present and the terrible ways in which time, redevelopment and the ravages of war have transformed a human environment into something strange and terrible' – Terence Brown. ●

Belfast Confetti

Suddenly as the riot squad moved in, it was raining exclamation
     marks,
Nuts, bolts, nails, car-keys. A fount of broken type. And the explosion
Itself – an asterisk on the map. This hyphenated line, a burst of rapid
     fire...
I was trying to complete a sentence in my head, but it kept stuttering,
All the alleyways and side-streets blocked with stops and colons.

I know this labyrinth so well – Balaclava, Raglan, Inkerman, Odessa
     Street –
Why can't I escape? Every move is punctuated. Crimea Street. Dead
     end again.
A Saracen, Kremlin-2 mesh. Makrolon face-shields. Walkie-talkies.
     What is
My name? Where am I coming from? Where am I going? A fusillade
     of question-marks.

Night Patrol

Jerking his head spasmodically as he is penetrated by invisible
    gunfire,
The private wakes to a frieze of pull-outs from *Contact* and *Men Only*.
Sellotape and Blu-Tack. The antiquated plumbing is stuttering that
    he
Is not in Balkan Street or Hooker Street, but in a bunk bed
In the Grand Central Hotel: a room that is a room knocked into
    other rooms.

But the whole Victorian creamy façade has been tossed off
To show the inner-city tubing: cables, sewers, a snarl of Portakabins,
Soft-porn shops and carry-outs. A Telstar Taxis depot that is a hole
In a breeze-block wall, a wire grille and a voice-box uttering
    gobbledygook.

Campaign

They had questioned him for hours. Who exactly was he? And when
He told them, they questioned him again. When they accepted who
    he was, as
Someone not involved, they pulled out his fingernails. Then
They took him to a waste-ground somewhere near the Horseshoe
    Bend, and told him
What he was. They shot him nine times.

A dark umbilicus of smoke was rising from a heap of burning tyres.
The bad smell he smelt was the smell of himself. Broken glass and
    knotted Durex.
The knuckles of a face in a nylon stocking. I used to see him in the
    Gladstone Bar,
Drawing pints for strangers, his almost-perfect fingers flecked with
    scum.

Cocktails

Bombing at about ninety miles an hour with the exhaust skittering
The skid-marked pitted tarmac of Kennedy Way, they hit the ramp
    and sailed
Clean over the red-and-white guillotine of the check-point and
    landed
On the M1 flyover, then disappeared before the Brits knew what
    hit them. So
The story went: we were in the Whip and Saddle bar of the Europa.

There was talk of someone who was shot nine times and lived, and
    someone else
Had the inside info. on the Romper Room. We were trying to
    remember the facts
Behind the Black & Decker case, when someone ordered another
    drink and we entered
The realm of Jabberwocks and Angels' Wings, Widows' Kisses,
    Corpse Revivers.

George Charlton

MOIRA CONWAY

Selection from: *Nightshift
Workers* (1989).

GEORGE CHARLTON was born in 1950 in
Gateshead, and now lives in Newcastle. In
1984 he was joint winner of the first Newcas-
tle *Evening Chronicle* poetry competition.

When a selection of his poems appeared
in the Bloodaxe anthology *Ten North-East
Poets*, *British Book News* admired his 'hon-
est social realism' and Douglas Dunn *(Times
Literary Supplement)* called him 'deft in rich
phrasing'. Most of the poems in his first col-
lection, *Nightshift Workers*, are set in North
East England: in the pubs, on the street,
down the allotments. ●

Nightshift Workers

They have come from a factory
Where fluorescent strips flared all night

And ears grew numb to machinery;
They are going home to working wives,

To cooling beds at breakfast time,
Undressing fatigue from their skin like clothes;

Later to wake at four and taste teeth
Soft as fur in their mouths.

They live in a dislocation of hours
Inside-out like socks pulled on in darkness

Waking when the day is over.
They are always at an ebb, unlike others

Going out to work in the morning
Where sun and moon shine in the sky together.

Gateshead Grammar

There must be hundreds like us now,
Born since the war, brought up
In terraced streets near factory yards
And on expansive council estates.

We were the ones who stayed on at school
In academic quarantine. Others
Took apprenticeships in the skilled trades,
And left us indoors to finish homework.

And we didn't notice it at first –
All the literature that wasn't written
For us: passing an exam
Was an exercise in its own right.

To live like Spartans, think like monks
Had something heroic about it...
Now we dress carefully, and at
Introductions in expensive restaurants

Suppress the local accent in our voice,
Not to give ourselves away.
And little by little we go home less
To parents who seem to have fostered us:

We are like those bankrupt millionaires
With our own social-success stories
And personal failures. Remaindered
Fashions at give-away prices.

Friday Evenings

The evening star sparks
Struck like a welding arc.

In dull light of the varnished pubs
Young men wait, scrubbed clean as water babies,

A faint idea of work dismissed
And leisure compromised.

Here and there a moustache soft as lichen
Moistens on the white head of a beer,

Cigarettes congest the ash-trays
Silted as their smoke-fouled mouths.

Mass participants in drink
These heroes of the commonplace

Anticipate the casual girls
The ever-expanding universe

Hurrying to a party,
Its platonic, its adulterated love.

Andrew Greig

MOIRA CONWAY

Selection from: *A Flame in Your Heart* (1986).

ANDREW GREIG was born in 1951 in Bannockburn, Stirlingshire. He is a mountaineer and freelance writer. He has published two books of poems with Canongate, *Men On Ice* and *Surviving Passages*, and two books on expeditions to Everest and the Karakoram Himalayas with Hutchinson.

His latest collection, *The Order of the Day* includes poems written during recent Himalayan expeditions. He worked with Kathleen Jamie on *A Flame in Your Heart*, a book of poems set in the summer of 1940 telling the story of the all-too-brief love of a Spitfire pilot, Len, and his girl, Katie. Some of Len's poems (written by Greig) appear below, some of Katie's in Kathleen Jamie's section (p. 89). ●

Len's poems

40

I went to visit Tim last night. He's a
little pale, but what do you expect.
He says thanks for the cigs and wants to book
'a slow smoochie with the poppet',
that is, a dance with you.
Says he'll be a little stiff but maybe
you could help with that. Winked. Swine!
I said I'm fighting to protect my girl
from hogs like you. 'Any excuse, old boy,
any excuse will do' – then an inward smile
quite at odds with his posh drawl
and that preposterous moustache...

We stood at the window in the dark,
sharing a cigarette as the bombers went over.
His hand shook on his stick, I helped him
to a chair. His hip is worse
than I'd realised, he'll not fly again.
'Well out of it' I said. Silence.
I'm a fool. You understand
I love the man. The far-off thud

of Bofors guns – shooting in the dark but
you have to put up some kind of a show.
He shook his head, lit up another,
never said a word.

I left with the All Clear, got a lift
from our Adjutant, he'd been visiting his son.
We didn't talk much. The night was clear,
there were many stars. I thought:
not all the faint ones are far away,
nor all the bright ones near,
some fuzzy things are galaxies.
It seemed important, I hung on to it
as the bitter smoke of Woodbine stung my eyes.

'Bloke next to Eddie died in the night,'
the Adj. said. 'Spare a fag?'
We hit something on the road.
'What was that?' 'Dunno, something small.'
We didn't stop. 'Well out of it, I reckon.'

I shook my head, lit up for two, passed one over.

51

I watch my tracers arc and seed
buds on the Heinkel's fuselage
and sheer off only when they rush to bloom
into one monstrous rose –
Death's gardener, that's me.
Good at it, too. The hands that touch you
turn green in the glow of instruments,
itching for employment in His estate...
Katie, as I write this I'm picturing
myself kneeling as I push peas
into mild earth with my forefinger,
somewhere in Hampshire, early March,
light rain falling...We will marry, won't we,
for whenever I see you now I feel
the urge to plant, deep and patiently.
Are you shocked or smiling? I can't tell.
But if I live, something must grow –
children, sweet peas, the dreaming marrow's

long ear pressed to the ground –
to screen off that mushrooming bloom.

(Only nothing will make it go away now.
Marry, yes, but if we're going to burn,
we'll burn. Garden of a lifetime
flowered and withered in a flash...)

Tony Flynn

TONY FLYNN was born in 1951 in Haslingden, Lancashire. He survived a strict Catholic education to read Philosophical Theology at Hull, and is now a social worker in Walsall.

His first collection, *A Strange Routine*, was widely praised: 'Short poems, lyrically underlined at moments of crisis... gaunt and lit by guilt' – Peter Porter. 'The delicacy and restraint with which Tony Flynn approaches his material of a working-class Catholic background in no way inhibit an extremely individual voice... An admirable, subtle and intelligent debut from a poet who gives considerable pleasure in the precision and resonance of his images' – Christopher Hope.   ●

Selection from: *A Strange Routine* (1980).

The New Dress

Undressing, her fingers find the zip,
and small teeth open along her spine.
She shivers, and can't resist
her mirror – the thrill as the blue
falls from her. She remembers
her cats...how their slack lope
bodies a cruel deceit – slit eyes
in the long grass, patient, murderous.
She dreams again the measured glide
of claw, the silent puncture's tiny bleb
of red at feathered throats – such skill.
She purrs, and steps from her silky pool.

Gerald Mangan

Selection from: *Waiting for the Storm* (1990).

GERALD MANGAN was born in 1951 in Glasgow, where he worked as a medical artist after leaving university. He has since lived as a poet, painter, illustrator and literary journalist in various parts of Scotland and Ireland, and has reviewed poetry and fiction for some years in *The Scotsman* and *Times Literary Supplement*.

During the mid-70s he worked as an actor and playwright at Theatre Workshop in Edinburgh, and later as writer-in-residence at Dundee College and Deans Community School, Livingston. He was awarded writer's bursaries by the Scottish Arts Council in 1978 and 1986. His first book of poems is *Waiting for the Storm*. ●

Glasgow 1956

There's always a headscarf stooped
into a pram, nodding in time
with a plastic rattle, outside a shop
advertising a sale of wallpaper.

There's a queue facing another queue
like chessmen across the street;
a hearse standing at a petrol-pump
as the chauffeur tests the tyres,

the undertaker brushes ash off
his morning paper, and my mother,
looking down at me looking up,
is telling me not to point.

The background is a level site
where we recreate the war.
Calder Street is Calder Street,
level as far as the Clyde.

Without a tree to denote it,
the season is moot. That faint
thunder is the Cathcart tram,
and the sky is white as a trousseau

posed against blackened bricks.
A grey posy in her hands,
the bride stands smiling there
for decades, waiting for the click.

Scotland the Ghost
(Tune: any bagpipe music)

It's no deid, the auld land, it's no deid in spirit:
All it wants is a stirrup-cup, and a coronach to stir it.
Drinking up at closing-time, it's girning in its chains:
O when, O floo'er o Scotland, will we see your like again?

It's no deid in spirit, no, it's never done with haunting;
But it never makes its mind up, to tell us what it's wanting.
The spirit's weak without the flesh, but still it lifts the hackles –
With its head below its arm-pit, and its ankle still in shackles.

It drags the sword of Wallace, it's lugging Bruce's helmet;
But spiders make their webs in it, and a draught would overwhelm it.
The heart inside the armour's like the queen inside her cell:
The breath of Knox has chilled it, and blasted it to hell.

The crown fell off with Jamie, when he took the English tiller;
The head fell off with Saltoun, who sold the tongue for siller.
When Bonnie Charlie dreamed his dream, to stick it back together,
He met a butcher's cleaver, and it ended up in slivers.

The heart grew black as Glasgow, then, and rumbled underground;
The disembodied head was known as Edinburgh town.
When Burns sprang up to sing of flesh, and earth, and barley-grain,
He sang too low, too late to touch the Socratean brain.

Sheriff Walter found the body stripped to bare essentials,
And shivering in the heather; but he saw its true potential.
He dressed it up in tartan plaid and kilt, for exhibition,
Installed it in his stately home, and charged them all admission.

Victoria had it dance a fling, and played it for a puppet –
A gillie on a string, without a *sgian dubh* to cut it.
Mass-produced in clockwork, it made the perfect vassal
To paint the atlas red for her, or dandle in her castle.

Burke and Hare worked double-time, supplying all the clients
Who analysed the body in the interests of science.
Doctor Jekyll knew the head was severed from the heart,
And drank a heady potion to explore the private parts.

MacDiarmid woke in a whisky haze, and saw a headless thistle –
Stuck his own on the prickly stalk, and sharpened up the bristles.
He kept the spirit neat and drank it deeply through a chanter,
Till the skull swelled beneath the skin, and stretched his Tam
      o'Shanter.

It's no deid, the auld land, it's no deid in spirit:
All it wants is a drunk man, and a World Cup to stir it.
In Gallowgate, in Canongate, it's girning in its pain.
It's watering the stones to make the floo'er bloom again.

Sean O'Brien

MOIRA CONWAY

Selection from: *The Indoor Park* (1983) and *The Frighteners* (1987).

SEAN O'BRIEN was born in 1952 in London. After living in Hull for many years, he moved to Brighton, and now teaches English at a comprehensive school in Crowborough. His first book of poems, *The Indoor Park*, a Poetry Book Society Recommendation, won him a Somerset Maugham Award. His second, *The Frighteners*, won a Cholmondley Award.

'Sean O'Brien's increasingly powerful and angry poetry confronts History head on, its shabbiness, its disgrace and its topical affronts. More so than in his brilliant first collection, *The Indoor Park*, he's found himself picking up a gauntlet that Thatcher's England has dropped at his feet' – Douglas Dunn. ●

The Snowfield
from THE INDOOR PARK

It is so simple, being lonely.
It's there in the silence you make
To deny it, the silence you make
To accuse the unwary, the frankly alone.
In the silence you bring to a park
When you go there to walk in the snow
And you find in the planthouse,
Next to the orchids in winter slow-motion
And sleeping unreadable mosses,
Sick men, mad, half-born, who are sitting
As long as the afternoon takes.
Left there by helpers hours ago,
As if preparing for a test,
Each holds a book he cannot open.

Some days you put together
Sentences to say for them
As you leave to go back to the street.
With work they might be epigrams
Of love and modest government.
And this thought frees you. You pick up the paper.
You eat. Or you go to the library and talk.

But some days there is nothing
You cannot know. You still leave,
But it seems to take hours, labouring
Back to the street through the snowdrifts
And not worth the effort.
It seems that this is all there is.
It happens like snow in a park, seen clearly
After days of admiration, and looking
As if it had always been there, like a field
Full of silence, that is not beginning or ending.
It is so simple. You just hadn't looked.
And then you did, and couldn't look away.

Song of the South
from THE FRIGHTENERS

We change our cars and eat our meat.
There are no negroes on our street.
Our sons are sailing with the fleet.
We keep our mania discreet.

We take our secretaries on trips.
We have a taste for furs and whips.
We look to Panama for ships.
It hurts us when the market slips.

We place our cash in Krugerrands.
We rule the waves, so say the bands
At Brighton, where we own the sands.
You won't find blood upon our hands.

Conservative in politics,
We have no time for lefty pricks
Who sympathise with wogs and spicks.
We print the kind of shit that sticks.

We even bought a moralist.
We fund his comic, keep him pissed.
Just now we need him to exist,
The sweaty little onanist.

It is of property we dream.
We like to think we are a team.
We think that poverty's a scream.
We're still more vicious than we seem.

And speaking of the next world war,
The bang we've all been waiting for,
We will survive: We are the law
That shuts and locks the shelter door.

Helen Dunmore

CLAIRE McNAMEE

Selection from: *The Sea Skater* (1986) and *The Raw Garden* (1988).

HELEN DUNMORE was born in 1952 in Beverley, Yorkshire. After graduating from York University in 1973, she worked in Finland for two years, and now lives in Bristol. Her second book of poems, *The Sea Skater*, won her an Alice Hunt Bartlett Award. Her third, *The Raw Garden*, is a Poetry Book Society Choice.

'Haunting poems . . . an elusive individuality sensitive to all changes in weather . . . She seems able to poach subliminal forebodings at will, and suddenly we are in that hallucinatory other-world, sharing her viewpoint' – *Poetry Review*. 'Gentle, humane poems which do not ignore the darknesses daily life is prone to overlook' – *The Independent*. ●

The bride's nights in a strange village
from THE SEA SKATER

At three in the morning
while mist limps between houses
while cloaks and blankets
dampen with dew

the bride sleeps with her husband
bundled in a red blanket,
her mouth parts and a bubble
of sour breathing goes free.
She humps wool up to her ears
while her husband tightens his arms
and rocks her, mumbling. Neither awakes.

In the second month of the marriage
the bride wakes after midnight.
Damp-bodied
she lunges from sleep
hair pricking with sweat
breath knocking her sides.
She eels from her husband's grip
and crouches, listening.

The night is enlarged by sounds.
The rain has started.
It threshes leaves secretively
and there in the blackness
of whining dogs it finds out the house.
Its hiss enfolds her, blots up
her skin, then sifts off, whispering
in her like mirrors
the length of the rainy village.

Seal run
from THE RAW GARDEN

The potatoes come out of the earth bright
as if waxed, shucking their compost,

and bob against the palm of my hand
like the blunt muzzles of seals swimming.

Slippy and pale in the washing-up bowl
they bask, playful, grown plump
in banks of seaweed on white sand,

seaweed hauled from brown circles
set in transparent waters off Easdale

all through the sun-fanned West Highland midnights
when the little potatoes are seeding there
to make necklaces under the mulch,
torques and amulets in their burial place.

The seals quiver, backstroking
for pure joy of it, down to the tidal
slim mouth of the loch,

they draw their lips back, their blunt whiskers
tingle at the inspout of salt water

then broaching the current they roll
off between islands and circles of oarweed.

At noon the sea-farmer
turns back his blanket of weed

and picks up potatoes like eggs
from their fly-swarming nest,

too fine for the sacks, so he puts them in boxes
and once there they smell earthy.

At noon the seals nose up the rocks
to pile there, sun-dazed,
back against belly, island on island,

and sleep, shivering like dogs
against the tug of the stream
flowing on south past Campbelltown.

The man's hands rummage about still
to find what is full-grown there.
Masts on the opposite shore ring faintly

disturbing themselves, and make him look up.
Hands down and still moving
he works on, his fingers at play blinded,
his gaze roving the ripe sea-loch.

Steve Ellis

Selection from: *Home and
Away* (1987).

STEVE ELLIS was born in 1952 in York, and
worked in the chocolate factory for two years
before going to University College, London,
where he later did his Ph.D. He is now a
lecturer in English at Birmingham Univer-
sity. His study *Dante and English Poetry* was
published by Cambridge University Press in
1983, and he is currently working on a verse
translation of Dante's *Hell*.

In 1982 he received a Gregory Award from
the Society of Authors, and in 1987 his first
collection, *Home and Away*, was published
by Bloodaxe. 'Ellis is very much a Bloodaxe
poet: toughly comic, anti-metropolitan,
often verbally exuberant' – John Lucas, *New
Statesman*. ●

The Age of Innocence

At school, we all had to pick a plague
out of Exodus; round the table,
elbowing each other in innocent enthusiasm,
the girls drew mostly feverish first-borns, the boys
boils and frogs; while I fancied the river of blood.
Except some little s-d had pinched all the reds.
So I did locusts: houses, palm trees, pyramids
carefully laid in; arabs arranged unsuspecting,
a sudden camel; stood back, aimed, and

FURIOUS blitzings with the pencil,
God's green pepper milling down,
marvellously missing Moses,
tucked with his rifle in the margin.
Our work went up round the walls, whereon
the headmistress appeared
in a clap of lavender,
benign and gratified,
and scattered gold stars like benedictions.

To Ted Hughes

While I was cooking dinner
(some friends were coming round)
I thought I'd try your new cassette.

But you know how it is –
pans and peeling to synchronise,
recipes, and then the phone ringing:

you faded into far-off noise,
a low drumming
seeping from the lounge.

So going in there was a shock –
like opening the door of an oven
on your simmering concerns,

the rolling prophetic growl
that preached its elementals
to our carpets and chairs

unheard, unattended. To resume
butchering the chicken
seemed an act of homage;

but to eat it afterwards
with cutlery, wine and conversation
an act of sneaking treachery.

We should have daubed each other
all over with it
and danced among the bones.

Marion Lomax

MOIRA CONWAY

Selection from: *The
Peepshow Girl* (1989).

MARION LOMAX was born in 1953 in Newcas-
tle, grew up in Northumberland, and now
lives in Berkshire. She gained her doctorate
from the University of York in 1983, and her
study of Elizabethan and Jacobean drama
was published by Cambridge University
Press in 1987.

In 1981 she received a Gregory Award,
and won first prize in the Cheltenham Festi-
val Poetry Competition with her poem *The
Forked Tree*. She was Creative Writing Fel-
low at the University of Reading in 1987-88,
and has lectured in English at St Mary's Col-
lege, Strawberry Hill since 1987. Her first
book of poems, *The Peepshow Girl*, was pub-
lished by Bloodaxe in 1989. ●

The Forked Tree

I killed two hares last night in the heart of the garden.
Long ears in moonlight, mimicking the shape of the tree.
I crept round the side of the house before they sensed me
And when they heard the gun clear its throat it was too late.
I hit the buck first, then the doe – stupidly standing
To stare at me. Her powerful hind-quarters refusing
To kick and run, though I knew she could have bounded up
The lane in an instant, back to her young. I can cope
With hares: they are easy to cook. I feel no remorse.
Now I'll wait for the vixen who raids the chicken house.

I feed my chickens. Gather and sort the eggs. I wipe
The dirt and straw collage from the shells of those I sell.
I have the dogs too. My husband trained them, but I was
Surprised how quickly they obeyed me. I talked to them –
More easily than I talked to the children. Could share
The shadow with its dark gun lurking by our house wall
And the silent bullet lodged inside before we knew
That it was growing. His coming out of hospital,
Then the sniper's second strike when he was off his guard.
In the end I could only stand stupidly and stare –

Even with warning, could not believe such treachery.
The children were swinging from the tree in the garden
With no one to catch them. Darkness made the ground tremble
With hooves which left the grass trampled and the roses spoiled.
I guard this warren – small rooms and scattered outbuildings.
Not even chickens shall live in fear of predators.
My children shall feed better than before. Lonely nights
Are not without fear, but I cope with darkness now that
I have seen it bring young deer down from the wood to play.
Jumping in and out in the moonlight, through the forked tree.

Jo Shapcott

DAVID HUNTER

Selection from: *Electroplating the Baby* (1988).

JO SHAPCOTT was born in London in 1953, and now works as Education Officer at London's South Bank Centre. In 1985 she won first prize in the National Poetry Competition with the poem *The Surrealists' Summer Convention Came to Our City*. The title-poem of her first book *Electroplating the Baby* (page 76) describes an experiment by a 19th-century French scientist who devised a way of mummifying bodies by giving them a metal coating.

'She turns the notion of privatisation and the private life inside out and plays all sorts of tricks with social consciousness, with politics, with history, with the imagination' – Tom Paulin. ●

The Surrealists' Summer Convention Came to Our City

We were as limp as the guidebooks
to the city. We had our ankle tendons
severed to combat the heat.
We dined on carp all summer:
the magazines were full of recipes.

The city fathers talked about a new guidebook
which would inform the tourists
in languages and dialects for all.
It was delightful in the streets
but there was outrage in the suburbs now that
it was no longer safe to stay in at night.

The carp was piquant but we were getting bored
picking out the lead shot. Some of the tourists
said it wasn't sporting. We got tired
of being barracked and decided to shock
by stringing violins with carp-gut.

The Philharmonia played especially sweetly that summer;
they made a recording of the Floral Dances
which is still controversial because of the sound
of chattering monkeys in the coda.

Weekends we shared dinner in our block, sitting
on the carpet and, by autumn, eating minced carp.

We ate carp with oranges and, retinas
stinging with zest, waited for the season to flop,
the mayor's lung complaint to become fatal,
the city's sheaf of stocks to falter.
But all that flopped that year were
the fishy moustaches on the breeding carp.

Photograph: Sheepshearing
Northlew, 1917

Here are six men, their tools, a cart,
a hedge with three trees breaking its smooth line.
Only half the men actually shear:
they have such control over those raggy piles
of sheep that they can still sustain
a hard stare out at us – not the modern, ironic
glance to camera, but a single-minded look
held for the full seconds needed to etch the image
on the photographic plate. In this way
they have looked themselves into my sphere.
Two boys man the hand-wound wheels
which drive the clippers. A tricky role:
to pose, frozen, while giving the impression
of vigorous wheel-turning. One is better at it.
The sixth character is the youngest boy.
He holds a sheep jammed against his upper legs,
its head in one hand, rump in the other.
This sheep will be the next for the clippers.
The anxiety of the two – the one for the shearing
of her fleece, the other for the enormity of his task
of staying stock-still for history –
is palpable in this one surprising
blur of fleece and features in the scene.
It is a fuzz of boy and sheep to set your teeth on edge:
a vibration to travel down to the bone.

Electroplating the baby

Of the Egyptians the rich alone
were capable of having it done.

The cadavers were immersed
in antiputrescible baths

and then swathed by the relatives
in thousands of bandages.

In our time the art of embalming
has not made much advance:

are our processes so imperfect
as to dull our inclination?

Or do we relish the privacy of dust?
In answer one physician proposes

electro-metallurgy as *the* way
to obtain indestructible mummies.

He metallises our entire cadaver.
He encloses it in an envelope

of bronze, copper, nickel, silver or gold
according to the wealth or caprice

of those who survive.
Does this waken your curiosity?

Do you wish to know
how Dr Variot proceeds?

In a double frame with four uprights
connected top and bottom by four square plates

is the body of a child which has been
perforated with a metal rod.

One end of the rod abuts
against the arch of the cranium

the other is inserted as a pivot
in a metallic bearing at the base of the frame.

The frame support is a conductor of electricity.
The uprights and connecting wires

are carefully insulated
with gutta percha.

The electric current is furnished
by three small "chaudron" thermo-electric batteries.

A circular toothed metallic contact
descends from the top plate and rests

lightly on the vertex of the cadaver.
The lower surface of the feet

and the palms of the hands
rest upon two contacts.

Before immersing this apparatus
in the electro-metallurgic bath,

it is necessary to render the body
a good conductor of electricity.

To this effect the operator
sprays the skin of the cadaver

with a solution of nitrate of silver
by means of a homely apparatus –

the atomiser used by ladies
for perfuming themselves.

This operation having been performed
the skin becomes of an opaque black

and the silver salt has penetrated
as far as to the derma.

Next the silver salt must be reduced:
that is to say, separated from its oxide

(to do this is very difficult).
The frame is placed under a glass bell

in which a vacuum has been formed,
and into which vapours of white phosphorus

dissolved in sulphide of carbon
are afterwards allowed to enter

(this is a dangerous operation
like all operations in which phosphorus

in solution plays any part whatever).
Then the skin of the cadaver

is of a greyish white.
There is nothing left to do now.

but to proceed as rapidly as possible
to the metallisation. To this effect

the frame is immersed in a bath
of sulphate of copper

(we need not describe this operation
which is known to all).

Under the influence of the electric current
the deposition of the metal goes on

uninterruptedly. The molecules
of metal deposit on the skin

and soon form thereon a continuous layer
(the operator must regulate

the passage of electricity with great care
in order to prevent a granular deposit

having but little adhesion).
By shifting the contacts properly

the operator will substitute for the skin
a coating of copper

which will take on the pattern
of all the subjacent parts.

By attentively watching
the thickness of the deposit

upon the face, hands and all
the delicate parts of the body,

a faithful mould will be obtained
that will exactly recall

the details of conformation
and the tints of the physiognomy.

A deposit of from half
to three quarters of a millimetre

offers sufficient strength
to resist external bendings and blows.

A thickness of from half
to three quarters of a millimetre

ought not to be exceeded
for the metallic covering

of the face and hands
which will be thus perfectly moulded.

Upon the trunk, the abdomen, the neck
and the first segments of the limbs

the integral preservation
of the plastic forms is much less important.

What is the future in store
for this process of mummification?

It would be impossible to say
it is infinitely probable

that metallised cadavers
will never figure

except in small numbers
for a long, long time to come.

Maura Dooley

MAURA DOOLEY was born in 1957 in Truro, Cornwall, and grew up in Bristol. From 1982 to 1987 she organised writers' courses at the Arvon Foundation's Lumb Bank centre in Yorkshire, and in 1987 became Literature Officer of London's South Bank Centre. She won a Gregory Award in 1987, and has published two short collections, *Ivy Leaves & Arrows* from Bloodaxe in 1986, and *Turbulence* from Giant Steps in 1988. *Money for Jam*, her first full-length collection, is due from Bloodaxe in 1991.

Selection from: *Money for Jam* (1991).

'Dooley shows an adventurousness, poise, range and sharpness of image that are lyrical, deeply-felt and wonderfully immediate' – *City Limits*. ●

Six Filled the Woodshed with Soft Cries

From grass-stained eggs we bred eight;
Two hens, six fine white cockerels,
They scrambled, fluffing feathers for
A summer and an autumn month.

Now, hands pinked by the wind,
I watch their maned necks nervously.
Yesterday the tiniest learnt to crow,
Latched a strange voice to crisp air,
His blood red comb fluting the wind,
Feathers creaming, frothing at his throat.

One month till Christmas, the clouds thicken,
He turns on me an icy, swivel eye,
Do you dare deny me?

My neighbour helps me chase them,
Snorting snuff, which rests on his sleeve
In a fine white scatter. A wicker basket
Gapes wide as he dives for them.
Six filled the woodshed with soft cries.
Their feathers cover stony ground
Like a lick of frost.

Neighbours

I'd been looking out for a loop of swallows
to tie up the end of those bitter months, when
you came carrying a litre of Chianti,
a packet of McVities Yoghurt Creams, a shovel
to bite into drifts of snow, a bag of salt to
throw at blue ice or over my shoulder
into the eyes of that devil, winter.

Months passed, seeing your headlights cross
the valley, a low thrum of engine heading home,
your washing line like a brave flag.
Spring was late, you dug through the dregs
of an old year, sawing and sowing. Things grew
and your bonfires sent more signals to me,
we're here, we're in, we're happy, busy.

It's you again today, your hands filled
with the last flowers of summer, asking me
about Yarrow. Achilles used the plant to soothe
the wounds made by weapons of iron (you know,
daggers through the heart). Take it,
let its green fingers bind with yours,
this valley is full of it.

And know that, like the swallows, when you go
you'll leave a small vibration in the air,
a nest for some cuckoo to fill.

Deborah Randall

DEBORAH RANDALL was born in 1957 in Gosport, Hampshire, and now lives in Kirkwall in the Orkneys. She worked in hotels, a plastics factory and a children's home before going to Sheffield University to study English, and only started writing three years ago. In 1987 she won the Bloodaxe poetry competition and the £1000 Bridport poetry competition, and saw her poems published in Penguin's *Gregory Poems* anthology. Her prize in the Bloodaxe competition was £1000 plus the publication of her first book of poems, *The Sin Eater*.

Selection from: *The Sin Eater* (1989).

Her poems are fiery, passionate and immediate. She is a new, original voice in contemporary British poetry. ●

Danda with a Dead Fish

Here is Danda with a dead fish,
This boy has too many limbs it seems,
More spindles than his running stitch can handle,
In from the green-flax sea-line with bare legs
And his knees clacking, chattering Danda
With a dead fish, what it is and whether fresh
Or not they'll pass it over, won't know,
Won't eat it she says, though you my dearie
Danda can have it for your supper, how
She teases, his big mother, navvie-built
To be a father; where do the men all go
When they have begot.

Don't look so starving Danda you
Little darling, who packs his food away
Like a navvie and is growing all slick
And silvery and smells kippery, he's been
Hull-picking with fishermen, his father was
One of them, nets going mouldy, Danda
Gets moods of the sea, and goose-bumps
Can't be scraped off, he'll get them again
On the shore, he lives there looking for

The man in him, they give
Tea and talk, slap him on the shoulder,
Call him fishy.

Danda's jumper unravelling, coming out
In sympathy, his nose is never cleanly,
Dripping brine all the time, scales under
His nails, always flexing, finding, bringing
In, a wind slaps hard on him singing up and
Down his ribs, Danda has no colour
Except of grey, the colour of
The day he lost his fiery ginger dadda
To the sea, except, his dadda really went away
With a woman not his mother;
Never mind our Danda, pass it over
Have your supper.

My Roaring Boy

My roaring boy comes home,
I hear him lungful across
the shifting corn, he scatters
the stooks and all before him, he is
bright as a cob's flank in June,
true as the ploughshare's chop
through the dark dark earth,
larger than the harvest moon
which is an owl's eye and cannot
lie and cannot deny his undoing
as the years fold and fold upon
themselves and his seed grows
to his overthrow and I do love him,
and he is, forever bright, forever
true, forever larger than the moon.
My boy comes roaring home.

Martin Stokes

MARTIN STOKES was born in 1958 in Mansfield. After reading English at Leeds University, he worked in Spain for six years, teaching English in Barcelona. He now lives in Chester where he teaches English to foreign students. He won an Eric Gregory Award in 1983. His first book of poems, *The First Death of Venice*, is a Poetry Book Society Recommendation.

Selection from: *The First Death of Venice* (1987).

'A confident, substantial and wide-ranging collection, with an air of exhilaration in the indulgence of impressive formal gifts. Appropriately for a poet, Stokes is drunk on words, a stylist and an experimenter. He is definitely one to watch' – Robert Johnstone, *Times Educational Supplement.* ●

She passed the test. He would not let her drive.

Her rising anger snapped taut.
She angered now for much more
than liberal female thought.
She'd won a pretext. A quick
and bad-tempered thing to score
him, strip of flex, hard plastic,
golden copper-wire core –

she snatched it from his proud car
and looped it round her wrist, rope
to grip in soft palms. So far
she'd only slapped in defence.
She had to make lemon-soap
smooth fingers grip down, go tense
and let him know. She could hope.

He saw her. He started back
and set his rushing mind high.
She advanced. Was that *his* knack
he saw her using? And on
she came towards him, to try.
She dared and sprang at his gone
feet and cracked the flex close by

his smaller bowed head. Cringe-eyed
he flinched aloud at that slap
of air. But he would not hide.
He parried with a short knife.
A white strip fell. The whip-snap
sang by and came back. His wife
brought down the ease of her trap.

He could only move a hand
in shy defence. The sharp flex
cut deeply. The girl could stand
over. She loved this. Loving
what an opened impulse checks,
what a tight-lipped grin could bring,
her freedom loved itself. No checks

for that or anything she might
now do to him. He bent, afraid
to jerk his knife, stand and fight.
She means it, he realised.
He felt the wound she had made.
She'd hurt him! He hadn't sized
her up at all. But he had paid

for all her things, hadn't he?
But the red wire whistled round
again, caught him suddenly.
Her wild mouth was also heard.
He stumbled low at the sound,
but stood. He'd been made absurd,
he knew. He watched the flex wound

less tightly in her tight grip.
The car at his back, he held
his knife up staff-like, a drip
of blood on the shaking skin
at the pointed end. She yelled
like Sioux or Samurai in
pleasure or in pain: he repelled

her. Obsessed by her own sake
she lashed the long wire out,
wrapped the blade and saw him take
her weapon up, away, and twist
it quickly from her. Without
the hard flex her whitened wrist
could not spin her anger out.

Her husband was so surprised
by his success, her next move
beat him. He lost his new-prized
winning knife. She simply kicked
it from his fingers. She wove
her hand in flex again, picked
up the hot knife too, and drove.

The Moehne Dam

'...another and intriguing way, thought Wallis
whimsically, of attacking the enemy at the source of
power.'   PAUL BRICKHILL, The Dam Busters

I.

A dam

defended by a heavy flak

emplacement, by searchlights,

and beautified

by ornamental pine trees.

A device designed high

and very thick, wide to withstand

stress, the pressure of its lake,   C

and pierced to let out part   O   R

of its catchment. Several pipes   N   A

diverted water for the Ruhr foundrymen   C   M

to drink and wash in. The volume of its depths   R   P

rewarded summer mornings, afternoons,   E   A

light evenings of quiet fishing, and maintained   T   R

high levels for the long, slow, heavy barges   E   T

heaving coal and iron through a network

of canals, delivering to foundries

for the manufacture of more tanks,

more locomotives, aircraft, guns,

more badges for distinguished service

and medals for acts of bravery,

such as bombing.

II.

Gone to flood the coal mines,
cover aerodromes, shut factories,
fuse the valley's hydro-electricity.
Water, pouring out, just gone

C
R   to damage forty-seven bridges
One   O
hundred   A   and re-align the railways.
   N
and thirty-four   M   The whole reservoir gone
million tons   to put its hands over bells and lights
of water   E   A   and drown a thousand people
gone.   R   (half of them were allied troops
   T   T   in a prison camp). Leaving behind
   E   a smell of mudbanks, boats, inverted fish,
a pair of ring-necked whooper swans
and other nesting rare birds.

Kathleen Jamie

IRENE REDDISH

Selection from: *A Flame in Your Heart* (1986) and *The Way We Live* (1987).

KATHLEEN JAMIE was born in 1962 in Renfrewshire, and won a Gregory Award at 19, which enabled her to travel in the Near East, and later to the Himalayas. She won Scottish Arts Council Book Awards for her short collection *Black Spiders*, published by the Salamander Press in 1982, and for her first full-length collection, *The Way We Live*, in 1988.

She worked with Andrew Greig on *A Flame in Your Heart*, a book of poems set in the summer of 1940 telling the story of the all-too-brief love of a Spitfire pilot, Len, and his girl, Katie. Some of Katie's poems (written by Jamie) appear below, some of Len's in Andrew Greig's section on page 57. ●

Katie's poems
from A FLAME IN YOUR HEART

16

Not what you'd imagine, not posh,
not Educated, bit silly, asks all the questions.
No moustache, more's the pity.
Not brave, I don't think. Said next to nothing
about flying (shame!) but left the glamour
to the loud-mouth yank (Canadian, actually)
who dribbled over Rosie. Not that
she cared, you know *her*. Anyhow

they threw about their money,
showed off, talked darts (I ask you!)
and histories. I suppose they can't
talk shop, we're trained Not to Get Involved –
so how do we Get Intimate? We didn't
want them to walk us home, you know,
said goodnight at the door
(doubt he'd ever kissed before!)

Shan't be long till he's posted
elsewhere. Sad really, he's sweet. (Confess:
said 'yes' to a date next week. Name's Len.)

35

He is 25, it is the last day
of his leave, and my whole world
rests gently against him. His arm
will tingle when he wakes! Keep peace,
keep still as the wallpaper birds
while the living take up their songs.
I feel the dawn of tenderness
I haven't known before. He's mine,
who can doubt it now morning shines
on us, on this aged mattress?
But the blue birds are painted forever
unmoved. We're young,
it's the last day of his leave. Wake him!

44

If you knew that little force
when I press stamps, then unthinking
watch my letter fall into the box...

That gentle touch
I feel beneath my ears
as you raise my face to yours...

I still kiss you, though I know
that soft pressing of the thumb
is all it takes to kill a man.

November
from THE WAY WE LIVE

He can touch me with a look
as thoughtless as afternoon
and think as much of hindering me
as he would of sailing away.

In November, when the storms come
he drums his fingers on his books and turns
them into a fist that crashes. On the shore

where he insists we walk, he holds me like a man
at a deck-rail in a gale. I suspect his eyes
are open, red and gazing over my head
in the direction of abroad.

I am left to tell him in a voice that
seems as casual as his talk of travel:
I think as much of leaving as
of forcing him to stay.

Petrol
from THE WAY WE LIVE

Sketch in the background: pre-dawn
in winter, snow on the hillsides,
marsh: brown-green, a winding
lochside road,
black ice.

It could have been
so much worse. No one was hurt.
As if you can care about
alternative universes
when this one gives trouble enough. O

that bonny smashed-up power-steering,
disc-brakes, axle,
front nearside suspension; no more
easy overnighting, end
of spinning our cash into petrol.

We must haul ourselves
out of the mire with help
from the keeper's tractor and none
whatsoever from the governors of fate,
who look down

on the scratch-marks, and smile.
Who look down on the petrol
spilled on the roadside
and smile.
It's business. It's tough.

The engine we'll resurrect, someday.
Tonight, hit the whisky
till we're split out through the spectrum:
as readily consumed, as volatile,
as figures etched in petrol.

Peter McDonald

PETER McDONALD was born in 1962 in Belfast.
He has been a Junior Research Fellow of
Christ Church, Oxford, and is now Fellow
in English at Pembroke College, Cambridge.
Selections of his poetry were published in
Blackstaff's *Trio Poetry 3* anthology in 1982
and in *New Chatto Poets* in 1986. He won
the Newdigate Prize in 1983, and an Eric
Gregory Award in 1987. His critical book,
Louis MacNeice: the poet in his contexts, was
published by Oxford University Press.

The poem *Silent Night* is based on the true
story of the imprisonment of Henri Le Druil-
lenec, of Jersey, in Wilhelmshaven (and,
afterwards, Belsen) in 1944-45. ●

Selection from: *Biting the
Wax* (1989).

Silent Night
St Aubin's Bay, Jersey, 1946

It's summer now, or nearly. Out at the back door, my sister
shows the children how to feed the birds, scattering pieces
of crust into the garden: some sparrows, a couple of starlings
come down and squabble, fly off at the children's applause.
In the bathroom, I'm weighing myself – another stone – smiling,
hearing my name called, catching the smells from the kitchen.

Those weeks when they came to take my story for the wireless
I had to be coaxed at first; they seemed to be after
more than names, or names and facts; they wanted to know
how it felt then, and sounded, what it tasted and smelt like,
though really it was like nothing, nothing before or since,
which I told them, and they understood, they said. But even so.

But even so, as they added, there was a story to be told,
and I was the man to tell it. First, there were questions
and answers, *What did you see then? And what were you thinking?*
But after a while, the story would come out of its own accord
and there were the details they wanted, the smells and the sounds,
memories that had never made sense, for once locking into each other.

The first place they took you. At Wilhelmshaven that winter,
when every afternoon repeated the frost of that morning
and at night there was only hail to cut into the tracks
of their lights, they bundled me with a couple of dozen
newcomers into one of the big huts, my feet touching
the ground for the first time since the court-martial in Jersey.

How many in this hut? There were nearly a thousand,
crammed three to a bed, head to toe in the bunks and making
barely a sound. Near enough a thousand men. Packed
that tightly, you soon learn how to sleep without moving,
and you learn not to speak, you learn to lie still and say nothing
when there are guards on hand to force up the value of silence.

It was part of Neue Gamme, and I'd been brought over
from France with the others – Jean De Frotté, Bernard
Depuy, just to give two names as examples: the first one
tall, wispy-haired and delicate, the son of a Marquis,
then Bernard with his square head screwed down on to his shoulders,
though they have their own stories, parts of mine and still different.

We had three things to think about: food, sleep and work,
but no real need to think, for they were all taken care of,
especially the last. Once a day, there was thin turnip soup
and a crust of bread, a few hours of motionless sleep,
then the hard tramp through frost out to the Kriegsmarine
Arsenal, a day's work hearing the punch and clang of the riveters,

avoiding the welders' blue clouds of sparks; sweat and iron;
then our convicts' shuffle back to the camp in the dark,
their searchlights tailing us and filling in the distance
back to the gates, our hut with its three hundred bunks.
I mentioned guards: there were guards of course, but worse
were the Chiefs, one to each hut. Ours was called Omar.

You might ask me to describe, explain him, but I can do neither,
I can tell you his build, his features, even mimic his voice,
but that would add up to nothing, or nothing more really
than just a man in a story, maybe a bit of a monster,
a dead man anyhow. Yes, by now he'll be safely dead.
It might be easier, really, for you yourself to explain him.

Omar, it turns out, had once, like most of the others,
been a prisoner himself, a young man when they caught him
in 1933, some kind of radical journalist.
He'd been through worse than this in his time, worse beatings,
work, cold and the rest, and he was in for a lifetime.
Drop by drop, I suppose, the fight just bled out of him.

So by the time the camps were getting busy they made him an offer,
to serve his time as an *Alteste* in places like Neue Gamme
with at least enough freedom there to do as he pleased
and get on with the job. Yes, the words apply, brutal, sadistic,
just like the others, inhuman. And yes, there are stories.
I try to remember my friend Bernard's straight talking,

'There's no point in judging a place like this by the standards
of what we've all left behind: it has a code of its own,
a lunatic code, I know, but you just have to learn it.
Lie still and say nothing.' So what is there for me to say now
about Omar? Just the truth, just what I remember?
But I couldn't call it the truth then, and now that I tell you

the stories, does that make them all true? does it make them
happen, happen properly for the first time? It's harder,
watching the sea relax under the first mild summer evening
and waiting for dinner, too, harder to force those things
to happen again, and here, than just to keep silent. And lie?
Here by the bay, there's really no such thing as silence,

what with the waves breaking all night, and the seabirds
carrying on as usual each day. On the wireless, they tell me,
you can do wonders, but the one thing you can't get away with
is silence, the fretful noise of empty spaces, the worrying
gaps bare of music or talk, with just the sound of the atmosphere
coming into your very own room. I can give you two stories

concerning Omar, though whether or not they go well together
I myself couldn't say. The first happened only a few weeks
after we arrived at the camp: an Alsatian boy of sixteen
had been caught making off with some scraps of food from the plates
of patients dying in the infirmary (though that was hardly a hospital
as you'd understand the word – a dirty, crowded tin hut).

He came up before Omar, of course, who glared and let his face buckle
in on itself with disgust, then brought out the worst of his voices,
the fabulously wicked giant, to himself above all.
'You, boy,' he thundered down, 'you have committed
the one unforgivable crime; you have gone out and stolen
not only from your comrades, but from your sick comrades.

I'll tell you exactly how you can expect to be punished:
you're going to be made to learn the real meaning of hunger,
but you'll dread the food in your mouth; and when you leave us
you'll be raving mad, boy, gibbering away somewhere to die.'
He was perfect. Large as life and more monstrous than any
caricature. We kept quiet; the boy cringed, was carried away.

The usual stamping, shouting and beating. Then the wet blankets
to sleep in as well, for nights on end. They starved him,
then force-fed him salted food, served up on a scalding
hot spoon, day after day, all the while refusing him water.
By the time they finally lost interest, he looked like a skeleton;
unable to eat for the burns on his mouth, his scarred lips and tongue,

he would scream at the sight of a spoon. He died soon, of course,
raving mad, as Omar had promised. Now I can barely imagine
such things happening at all, but they did, and do still
in theory, in places far removed from this island,
the standard horrors, common knowledge now more than ever,
more than just hearsay these days: newsreels, words on the air.

And then of course there's the second *vignette*: the very same Omar –
who was, needless to say, cultured, had once been a classical
musician, to add to his attributes, always a lover of Mozart –
in the Christmas of '44, Omar's treat for the prisoners.
Imagine one of the huts that's been specially cleared for the purpose,
with benches there now and a stage, the audience all silent

(though you'd hardly mistake that silence for hushed expectation,
it being clearly enough the schooled silence of fear)
and then you make out a Christmas tree just to the right of the stage,
a piano likewise, the feeling of something about to begin.
Then suddenly Omar and the six other *Altesten*
troop on like schoolboys, heavy, bloated, all with straight faces.

For this is the carol service, and these fat men are the carollers.
Listen and you'll pick up easily Omar's gentle booming
among all the voices here. In fact I myself was arrested
for 'communal listening'; the whole thing happens again for the
        wireless,
but no actor alive could reproduce the sound of this memory,
that music in the hungry air, *Stille nacht, Heilige nacht.*

On clear evenings, I watch those rocks on the near side of the bay,
a circle of broken teeth, finally blotted out by the tide.
I listen to seabirds roosting for miles along the whole coastline,
and then there's just the sea noise and the evening programmes
with the bad and the good news, the music of Victor Sylvester,
the Epilogue, the King, the whisper and fizz of the atmosphere.

Some nights I almost see the dead and the living stand in a circle,
naked but for their memories, and in full view of each other,
immobile as those rocks crumbling gradually into the bay,
as though they were trying to speak, or cry, or scream in the silence,
to hear each other and understand; but the dead weight of stone
holds us all down, makes us stand still and say nothing.

But not when they call me to dinner, and I laugh with the children
over this or that story, though sometimes I'll catch myself thinking,
not of the past exactly, but more of that programme,
my voice and the voices of actors, and somewhere among them
Jean and Bernard alive; Omar's Christmas carol; the last
winter of a bad war; a boy with a horror of spoons.

Simon Armitage

MOIRA CONWAY

Selection from: *Zoom!*
(1989).

SIMON ARMITAGE was born in 1963 in Huddersfield and grew up in West Yorkshire. He works as a probation officer in Oldham, and lives in Marsden, near Huddersfield.

He won an Eric Gregory Award in 1988, and has published three pamphlets: *Human Geography* (Smith/Doorstop, 1986), *The Distance Between Stars* (The Wide Skirt, 1987), and *The Walking Horses* (Slow Dancer Press, 1988). His work has appeared in many magazines, including *The Echo Room*, *Harry's Hand*, *London Magazine*, *The North* and *The Wide Skirt*. His first book-length collection *Zoom!* (1989) won a Poetry Book Society Choice, and was shortlisted for the Whitbread Prize. ●

Very Simply Topping Up The Brake Fluid

Yes, love, that's why the warning light comes on. Don't
panic. Fetch some universal brake-fluid
and a five-eighths screwdriver from your toolkit
then prop the bonnet open. Go on, it won't

eat you. Now, without slicing through the fan-belt
try and slide the sharp end of the screwdriver
under the lid and push the spade connector
through its bed, go on, that's it. Now you're all right

to unscrew, no, clockwise, you see it's Russian
love, back to front, that's it. You see, it's empty.
Now, gently with your hand and I mean gently,
try and create a bit of space by pushing

the float-chamber sideways so there's room to pour,
gently does it, that's it. Try not to spill it, it's
corrosive: rusts, you know, and fill it till it's
level with the notch on the clutch reservoir.

Lovely. There's some Swarfega in the office
if you want a wash and some soft roll above
the cistern for, you know. Oh don't mind him, love,
he doesn't bite. Come here and sit down Prince. Prince!

Now, where's that bloody alternator? Managed?
Oh any time, love. I'll not charge you for that
because it's nothing ᵣf a job. If you want
us again we're in the book. Tell your husband.

Ten Pence Story

Out of the melting pot, into the mint;
next news I was loose change for a Leeds pimp,
burning a hole in his skin-tight pocket
till he tipped a busker by the precinct.

Not the most ceremonious release
for a fresh faced coin still cutting its teeth.
But that's my point: if you're poorly bartered
you're scuppered before you've even started.

My lowest ebb was a seven month spell
spent head down in a stagnant wishing well,
half eclipsed by an oxidised tuppence
which impressed me with its green circumference.

When they fished me out I made a few phone calls,
fed a few meters, hung round the pool halls.
I slotted in well, but all that vending
blunted my edges and did my head in.

Once, I came within an ace of the end
on the stern of a North Sea ferry, when
some half-cut, ham-fisted cockney tossed me
up into the air and almost dropped me

and every transaction flashed before me
like a time lapse autobiography.
Now, just the thought of travel by water
lifts the serrations around my border.

Some day I know I'll be bagged up and sent
to that knacker's yard for the over spent
to be broken, boiled, unmade and replaced,
for my metals to go their separate ways...

which is sad. All coins have dreams. Some castings
from my own batch, I recall, were hatching
an exchange plan on the foreign market
and some inside jobs on one arm bandits.

My own ambition? Well, that was simple:
to be flipped in Wembley's centre circle,
to twist, to turn, to hang like a planet,
to touch down on that emerald carpet.

Those with faith in the system say 'don't quit,
bide your time, if you're worth it you'll make it.'
But I was robbed, I was badly tendered.
I could have scored. I could have contended.